Your
Horoscope
2020

....

Scorpio

Your Horoscope 2020

....

Scorpio

24th October - 22nd November

igloobooks

igloobooks

Published in 2019
by Igloo Books Ltd
Cottage Farm
Sywell
NN6 0BJ
www.igloobooks.com

0819 001.01
2 4 6 8 10 9 7 5 3 1
ISBN 978-1-78905-718-8

Written by Belinda Campbell and Denise Evans

Cover design by Dave Chapman
Edited by Bobby Newlyn-Jones

Printed and manufactured in China

CONTENTS
. . . .

INTRODUCTION
....

This horoscope has been specifically created to allow
you to get the most from astrological patterns and
the way they have a bearing on not only your zodiac
sign, but nuances within it. Using the diary section
of the book you can read about the influences and
possibilities of each and every day of the year. It will
be possible for you to see when you are likely to be
cheerful and happy or those times when your nature
is in retreat and you will be more circumspect. The
diary will help to give you a feel for the specific
'cycles' of astrology and the way they can subtly
change your day-to-day life.

THE CHARACTER OF THE SCORPION

....

Highly intimate, transformative, and controlled, Scorpios are the seducers of the zodiac calendar that are hard to resist. Whilst the affection of a Scorpio can be addictive, their passion can quickly feel possessive, so don't enter a serious relationship with this intense sign lightly. If you get on the wrong side of this powerful sign, whether it's by hurting them or someone that they fiercely love, then prepare yourself for an almighty sting from this Scorpion's tail; just as their love is unforgettable, so is their scorn. Associated with the genitals, Scorpios may struggle to separate themselves from their sexy reputation, however private they keep their love lives.

Scorpios are perhaps the deepest of all the Water signs and so can require some extra patience and searching to get to the core of their mysterious self. Scorpios have a negative energy that means that most of their emotions will be kept internal, however, they might like to express their emotions through writing, like Scorpio poet and novelist, Sylvia Plath. This sign doesn't like to allow itself to be vulnerable, (remember their rather sensitive associated part of the body), so trust and loyalty may be hard won. This Scorpion is quick to protect themselves and their loved ones from any harm so may keep their armour up until they decide it's safe to let someone in.

Born in the middle of autumn, Scorpio is a fixed sign that may enjoy security and can be single-minded in their approach towards reaching their goals. Co-ruled by Mars and Pluto, these astrological bodies give Scorpios a controlled and competitive attitude that will generally mean that they end up getting what they want out of life once they set their mind to it; take the three Scorpio Jenners, model Kendall, momager Kris, and transgender Caitlyn, as perfect examples of Scorpio's sexiness, controlling nature, and ability to transform.

THE SCORPION

Terrifying for most people to behold, the venom in their tail perhaps not helping, the Scorpion has a fierce reputation that some Scorpios can most certainly live up to, however, there is so much more to this creature than just their sting. Throughout a scorpion's life, it will shed its exoskeleton when it becomes too small and emerge larger and more powerful than before. Scorpios may experience a similar transformation within their lifetime, whether it's shedding their childhood as they move away to university, deciding on a change in career in their later years, or an internal transformation of some kind. Whilst the scorpion and Scorpio go through these changes they can be at their most vulnerable as their new-found selves fully form. However, once the transformation is complete both will reveal themselves stronger and more powerful than before. The scorpion is a predatory and defensive creature. Just like a Scorpio, they can go after what they want and are prone to lash out if they feel confronted. A nocturnal animal, Scorpios may also enjoy plenty of partying on nights out in their younger years; find them in the clubs shining under the ultraviolet lights like the mysteriously glowing scorpion!

PLUTO AND MARS

Renamed a dwarf planet in 2006, Pluto co-rules the sign of Scorpio with Mars. Pluto's demotion has made it no less mysterious to onlookers and its secrets are yet to be fully understood, which makes it a fitting ruler for the secretive Scorpio. Named after the Roman God of the Underworld, Pluto (Hades in Greek Mythology), this planet is associated with power and depth, just like the emotionally deep and controlling sign of Scorpio. The measured power from Pluto teamed with Scorpio's other ruling planet, Mars, makes for a sign that has controlled energy with plenty of drive and fight. Named after the Greek God of war, Mars is linked with passion and can feed into a Scorpio's possessive and sensuous nature. From Mars, Scorpios can find the courage to go after what they desire, both in their personal and professional lives. Born in the eighth house in the zodiac calendar, which is associated with regeneration, the power of Pluto and the strength of Mars means that Scorpios can hold huge potential for transformation and may choose to reinvent themselves several times over.

ELEMENTS, MODES AND POLARITIES

Each sign is made up of a unique combination of three defining groups: elements, modes and polarities. Each of these defining parts can manifest themselves in good and bad ways and none should be seen to be a positive or a negative – including the polarities! Just like a jigsaw puzzle, piecing these groups together can help illuminate why each sign has certain characteristics and help us find a balance.

ELEMENTS

Fire: Dynamic and adventurous, signs with Fire in them can be extroverted. Others are naturally drawn to them because of the positive light they give off, as well as their high levels of energy and confidence.

Earth: Signs with the Earth element are steady and driven with their ambitions. They make for a solid friend, parent or partner due to their grounded influence and nurturing nature.

Air: The invisible element that influences each of the other elements significantly. Air signs will provide much-needed perspective to others with their fair thinking, verbal skills and key ideas.

Water: Warm in the shallows and freezing as ice. This mysterious element is essential to the growth of everything around it, through its emotional depth and empathy.

MODES

Cardinal: Pioneers of the calendar, cardinal signs jump-start each season and are the energetic go-getters.

Fixed: Marking the middle of the calendar, fixed signs firmly denote and value steadiness and reliability.

Mutable: As the seasons end, the mutable signs adapt and give themselves over gladly to the promise of change.

POLARITIES

Positive: Typically extroverted, positive signs take physical action and embrace outside stimulus in their life.

Negative: Usually introverted, negative signs value emotional development and experiencing life from the inside out.

SCORPIO IN BRIEF

The table below shows the key attributes of Scorpio. Use it for quick reference and to understand more about this fascinating sign.

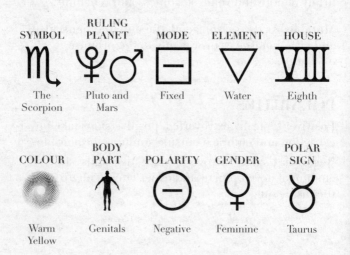

SYMBOL	RULING PLANET	MODE	ELEMENT	HOUSE
The Scorpion	Pluto and Mars	Fixed	Water	Eighth

COLOUR	BODY PART	POLARITY	GENDER	POLAR SIGN
Warm Yellow	Genitals	Negative	Feminine	Taurus

LOVE

When it comes to Scorpio's relationships, there is no dipping your toe in with this Water sign, their love is more like plunging head first from the highest diving board. The intensity of sexpot Scorpio's affection can be scary for some and less-daring signs may feel intimidated by their passion, but those that are brave enough to take the plunge will be rewarded with Scorpio's exhilarating and all-consuming love. A Scorpio might have their partners jump through some hoops to test their loyalty, but it's only to see if they are as serious about the relationship as the Scorpio is; only then will Scorpios really open up to their partners. When Scorpios fall in love it is truly, madly, and deeply with their heart, body, and soul.

In a long-term relationship, this fixed sign can have a steadfast approach to the one they love; there's nothing fickle about Scorpio's feelings. A committed Scorpio is loyal and protective and will always come to their partner's defence. Potential partners will be attracted to sexy Scorpio's charisma and enigmatic charm, but only the lucky ones will know Scorpio's deepest secrets and feelings as this secretive sign will only share these with a chosen few in their lifetime. Once a Scorpio lays claim to their chosen partner, their passionate love can turn into an obsessive jealousy if they're not careful.

With the influence of Pluto, Scorpios may experience some power struggles in their relationships and with their warring planet of Mars guiding them, disagreements can turn into a battlefield if emotions run high. Possessive Scorpios should try to resist controlling their partner and give them as much autonomy in the relationship as necessary, especially with individualist and free-spirited signs like Aquarius and Sagittarius. Regardless of what has set Scorpio to attack mode, if a Scorpion is arguing with their lover it is because they think they are worth fighting for. If you are an angered Scorpio or fighting with one, try to turn that intensity into passion rather than rage.

ARIES: COMPATIBILITY 2/5

If it's passion Aries desires in a relationship, a Scorpio could be the perfect sign for romance. However, this match might be too controlling and combative for long-term happiness. Both ruled by the planet Mars, these two may come into this relationship armed and ready to fight. Scorpio's controlling and jealous tendencies could be a source of many of these steaming fights with this Water sign. If this Fire and Water duo can work out a balance of control and ease the Scorpio lover's jealousy, then these two could have one steamy relationship rather than being left hot and bothered.

TAURUS: COMPATIBILITY 5/5

Scorpio and Taurus are each other's opposites on the zodiac calendar so cosmically share a special relationship both in their differences and similarities. The element of Taurus is Earth and Scorpio's Water which usually will mean that both partners will provide something that the other desperately needs. Love and passion are both driving forces for these two. Scorpio has the reputation for being the sexiest of signs and Taurus the most beautiful, so a physical relationship should be strong here. Whilst this couple will no doubt enjoy each other's bodies, their tendencies towards possession and jealousy will need to be kept in check.

GEMINI: COMPATIBILITY 3/5

Passionate debates could be on the menu for a Scorpio and Gemini love affair. The Water sign of Scorpio will bring emotional depth to the relationship whilst a Gemini's Air influence will help breathe a fresh perspective on things. Scorpios risk suffocating Geminis with their intense emotions if turned toxic. Geminis can be flirtatious which can trigger Scorpio's jealousy, but Geminis aren't scared of a little arguing, in fact they quite like the stimulation. Being a fixed sign, Scorpios value steadiness so may find flighty Gemini too unreliable, however, this relationship has the potential to be full of spice and interest.

CANCER: COMPATIBILITY 2/5

These two Water signs can easily get lost in each other's emotions. Ruled by Mars, Scorpio's passion for their Cancerian lover will be intense and a Cancerian will likely be highly attracted to a sensual Scorpio. Both the Scorpion and Crab can be stubborn and unwilling to bend to their partner's wishes if they don't match their own. Claws and stingers at the ready, disagreements could see both sides getting hurt and might end with them parting ways quickly. However, once these two decide that they want to be together, they can experience a love that is unfailing in its loyalty.

LEO: COMPATIBILITY 1/5

The love between Water sign Scorpio and fiery Leo can be one of deep intimacy or dampened spirits. Here are two fixed signs that could clash in their different approaches and refuse to yield to each other's strong personalities. Shared assets, particularly money, could prove difficult for a Scorpio and Leo. Scorpio is born in the eighth house where shared possessions are important, and Leos belong in the fourth house where a love of gambling lives which could result in conflict for the couple. If respect is exercised regularly between these two lovers, theirs is a closeness well worth protecting.

VIRGO: COMPATIBILITY 5/5

Placed two apart on the zodiac calendar, the passionate and loyal bond between the Virgin and Scorpion is a special one. Orderly Virgos will value the steadiness of a fixed sign Scorpio, and similarly the loyal Scorpio will appreciate the faithfulness that many Virgos are known for. With their complimentary elements of Water and Earth and their matching negative energies, this typically introvert couple will enjoy the nourishing effects of spending quality time with each other. Theirs is an intimate relationship but not without some passionate arguments thanks to power ruled Scorpio's influence of Pluto and Virgo's sharp tongue.

LIBRA: COMPATIBILITY 2/5

When the planets align for Scorpio and Libra, the combination of loving Venus, passionate Mars, and powerful Pluto can make for an intimate and stimulating love affair. The emotions of a Water sign and mindfulness of Air can be a harmonious pairing so long as a Scorpio and Libra are on the same page. Libras can feel superficial to the deep feeling Scorpio, but thankfully when this head and heart ruled couple fail to understand each other, Libra's charm and diplomacy can help calm any troubled waters. This love won't be without conflicts, sorry Libra, but it could be loyal and long-lasting.

SCORPIO: COMPATIBILITY 4/5

Was there ever a couple more deeply and desperately devoted to one another than Scorpio and Scorpio? The intimate connection that these two mysterious introverts can make is both in mind and body. They both can be guilty of passionate outbursts, particularly with jealousy, and their fixed attitudes can lead to arguments if they can't agree. If these two can patiently hold their breath in stormier times then this is a relationship that could sail off into the sunset together. Scorpio and Scorpio are a true power couple that thanks to their hardy Scorpion nature can withstand plenty.

SAGITTARIUS: COMPATIBILITY 2/5

Sagittarius and Scorpio can have a daring partnership;
whether their gamble on each other pays off is another
thing entirely. The adventurous Sagittarian will help
expand Scorpio's horizons and appeal to their brave
side, whilst Scorpio's fixed attitude can teach the flaky
Sagittarian to stay motivated and see things through.
The love of Scorpio can be all encompassing and the
worst thing for a Sagittarian is for them to feel like their
partner is at all possessive. This is definitely not a boring
love, but flexibility and growth are both key for these
two getting the most out of the relationship.

CAPRICORN: COMPATIBILITY 5/5

When Capricorn and Scorpio set their sights on each
other, these highly dedicated signs could be in it for the
long run. Placed two apart on the Zodiac calendar, theirs
is a devout bond that is likely to be highly compatible
with matching negative energies, complementary
elements, and harmonising cardinal and fixed modes.
A Capricorn can offer the security that Scorpio desires
and Scorpio can be the powerful influence that feeds
Capricorn's ambition. Scorpio will bring the fun and
Capricorn will bring the itinerary to go with it. If they
can take it in turns to rule the roost, their love could go
the distance.

AQUARIUS: COMPATIBILITY 1/5

Mysterious Scorpio and unique Aquarius may well find themselves attracted to one another, but the Scorpion and Water Bearer may need to work hard to keep their relationship off the rocks. Positive Aquarians are outgoing, and socialising in their communities is important, but this contrasts with introverted Scorpios who tend to have a small and intimate circle of friends. Their modes are both fixed which means they can be resistant to changing their contrasting outlooks. If stable Scorpio can embrace this Air sign's free-spirited nature and rational Aquarius can provide the intimacy that Scorpio needs, then these two could find their happiness.

PISCES: COMPATIBILITY 4/5

Here are two Water signs that will go to the ends of the Earth, or rather the depths of the oceans for one another. Pisceans dream of finding that fantasy love and the enigmatic Scorpio can be just that for them, whilst the empathetic Pisces can be the kindred spirit that secretive Scorpios can finally be vulnerable with. A Piscean's mutable nature, that flows with change can be at odds with the steadfast approach of a fixed Scorpio, but their differences mean that they have plenty to learn from each other. Emotional security and sensitivity are where these two thrive.

FAMILY AND FRIENDS

The negative energy in Scorpios means that this sign is quite happy to spend time alone, however, even if they do not actively seek out new friendships, the bonds that this sign will make are extremely important to them. Scorpio's group of friends is likely to be small as they value quality over quantity. Each friend of a Scorpio will have been carefully selected and may have gone through vigorous tests set by their Scorpion comrade to prove their worthiness. The reason for Scorpio's caginess comes back to their fear of letting their guard down and exposing themselves to pain; trust is an important practice for any Scorpio who wants to experience the benefits of close friendship.

As with most relationships, whether it be friends or family, finding common interests is key to forming and maintaining bonds. Secretive Scorpions could adore a good mystery, so a day out solving an escape room or a night in discussing this month's thriller book club choice could be two great ways for a Scorpio to bond with their suspense-seeking friends; Virgo's methodical analysis could make them the perfect partner for helping Scorpios get to the bottom of a crime or an extrovert Leo friend will no doubt jump at the chance to arrange a murder mystery in a spooky house for all of their friendship group to enjoy.

Another passion of sumptuous Scorpio is food and drink, whether it be opening an expensive bottle of wine at home or enjoying the tasting menu at the latest Michelin star restaurant in town. Scorpio's negative energy could have them spending all day at home, whipping up a gluttonous feast for their family and friends to enjoy, whom likely will be quite familiar with Scorpio's culinary talents. Venus ruled signs Libra and Taurus are friends that will happily indulge in Scorpio's love for luxury and will probably be the ones bringing over the bottles of champagne to their Scorpio host.

Scorpios can be emotionally intuitive parents; if there is something amiss with Scorpio's child, or any family member, this sign could readily pick up on it and be set on fixing whatever the problem is for their loved one. The Scorpion's love for their family is intense and their protective nature is formidable to challenge, so loved ones should rest assured that Scorpio has their back through thick and thin. The possessive and jealous side of a Scorpio could rear its unsightly head when it comes to those that this sign treasures most. Scorpio will indeed love their family like treasure and they will no doubt be the most valuable thing in this sign's life, but they should avoid treating people like possessions and trust their family to always return to them. Empowering their friends and family rather than using their own power over them will be key in maintaining happy and successful relationships for Scorpio.

MONEY AND CAREERS

· · · · · · · · · · · · · · · · · · ·

Being a certain star sign will not dictate the type of career that you have, although the characteristics that fall under each sign could help you identify the areas in which you could potentially thrive. Conversely, to succeed in the workplace, it is just as important to understand what you are good at as it is to know what you are less brilliant at so that you can see the areas in which you will need to perhaps work harder to achieve your career and financial goals.

Committed Scorpios aren't inclined to flit between jobs, unless they are still figuring out what they want to set their mind to. Scorpio's immense dedication may well see them stay in the same job or working for the same company for many years, whether they are 100% happy in it or not. A Scorpio devoted to their career should make sure that it comes from a place of passion rather than complacency. Scorpios can value security above their job satisfaction, and if they fear failure then they may decide to not try anything too daring. Channelling the influence of Mars, Scorpio should dare to dream and actively chase after their career goals with courage.

Scorpio's single-minded approach to life can mean that they lose themselves obsessively in their work, so it helps if they are passionate about their career. A sign as mysterious as Scorpio will often be attracted to the obscure or shadowy and won't shy away from darker occupations. Whether it's making an indie horror film inspired by fellow Scorpio Martin Scorsese, writing a thriller novel, or working in a funeral home, what might give other people nightmares could be the Scorpion's career calling.

Scorpios tend to be very private, especially when it comes to their bank accounts; asking a Scorpio about their salary could feel like asking them to strip down to their underwear. However, it might be clear from Scorpio's lavish spending habits as to how well they are doing financially. High earning jobs certainly will suit the shopaholic Scorpio who enjoys treating themselves to the very best of everything. Remember, this sign is about quality over quantity so whilst their shopping bags may be few, what lays inside them is likely to be of high value. The secrecy around spending and their funds may mean that they choose to keep some of their finances under wraps, even from their spouses.

Whilst you can't always choose who you work with,
it can be advantageous to learn about colleagues' key
characteristics through their star signs to try and work
out the best ways of working with them. Hardworking
Capricorns can bring structure and order to the work
life of a Scorpio and make sure their passion for a
project does not fizzle out before it has reached fruition.
Signs with a strong influence of Mercury, like Virgo and
Gemini will offer their thoughts and opinions willingly
to a Scorpio seeking advice and can be important
colleagues to bounce ideas off.

HEALTH AND WELLBEING

. . . .

The scorpion is known for being able to withstand almost anything, freeze this creature solid and then thaw it out and this durable wonder can still be alive! Similarly, Scorpios (minus the freezing bit) can endure serious hardship and deep emotional grievances. These folks are certainly made of hardy stock, but their Water element can make them feel pain deeper than most and make their inner power hard to channel at times. Scorpios are undoubtedly strong, but their tendency to isolate themselves in times of stress can sometimes weaken them as they close themselves off to any outside support. This controlling sign may struggle to ask for help and allow their vulnerability to be exposed but asking for help is never a sign of weakness and should only help strengthen Scorpio.

When a stressed-out Scorpion is feeling overwhelmed, they can turn to escapism for an immediate solution to their problems; binging on box sets, wrapped up in a blanket, and still wearing their pyjamas may be a familiar scenario. Whilst cocooning themselves away like this, with a trashy movie, may feel initially comforting they should be careful of doing this too regularly as it could also start to have the reverse effect. Losing themselves in a good book or spending time with an Aries or Leo friend who they have not seen in a while and will be happy to talk about themselves for an hour or two could be a far more positive distraction. Hearing about the problems of others may give some healing perspective to Scorpio's own issues, or at the very least will strengthen their friendship ties and make both parties feel happier from having taken the time to catch up.

Whilst this sensitive sign may be the best of all the Water signs at controlling their emotions thanks to the influence of Pluto, Scorpio's sting of aggression will usually pierce their victim with the strongest of venom. Fortunately for everyone, this Scorpion's scorn is usually infrequent, but trying to avoid big bursts of aggression is still an important lesson for this sign to learn. Scorpios can have a wonderful sense of humour, so trying to channel a lighter mood that allows them to laugh at life rather than going on the attack will hopefully diffuse any internal aggression from building up. Scorpions are intense by nature and their serious side is dominant but inviting fun into their lives and not taking things too seriously should help to balance out their moods.

With the influence of Mars and Pluto, Scorpio can have a lot of powerful energy that if left unreleased can cause emotional and physical discomfort. Teamwork isn't always a Scorpio's forte, their negative energy and fixed mode lends itself well to working alone, however, a little healthy competition can really fuel Scorpio's energy; signing up to a running or swimming race could rid Scorpio of their restless energy and set positive goals for them. If it's a surplus of emotional energy that is building up in this Water sign, then finding ways to sensitively release what is inside of them is also imperative; writing poems or a novel could be a positive outlet for this emotional sign as well as always seeking out professional therapy if necessary.

Scorpio

· · · · · · · · · · · · · · ·

2020
DIARY PAGES

JANUARY

. . . .

Wednesday 1st

Happy New Year! The Moon is in your creativity sector meaning that this is a good time to express your deepest wishes. Mars, one of your ruling planets, is nearing the end of his stay in Scorpio and is urging you to bring a project to completion. You have more energy and drive now.

Thursday 2nd

There may be much communication and racing around paying people short visits today. Egos may become inflated, but it will all be in good taste. Santa is still around bringing joy and making people laugh. Remember to stop for a breath. This is a jolly time with many stories shared amongst family.

Friday 3rd

The Moon moves into your health and duties sector today. Elsewhere, Mars, on the final degree of Scorpio, is encouraging the necessity of endings while the Moon takes care of new beginnings. You may be starting a new job, routine or health regime. Resolutions made now will probably be kept all year.

Saturday 4th

Mars moves into your money sector today. This is good news for you, as he is known for going after what he wants and getting it. Finances will improve because you have more motivation now. Just beware not to be ruthless and selfish with money or it could be taken away just as easily.

Sunday 5th

Taurus is where your relationship sector lies, and this area is also where you project your shadow onto others. You are the master of projection and this can make important relationships very complex. The Moon is in this area today, which can bring out the best and the worst in you.

Monday 6th

Today brings a chance to view relationships through a lens of learning. Researching psychology will give you the edge in dealing with difficult people. Sometimes you forget this, and your secretive nature can lead you to probe for other people's secrets. Be careful not to overstep boundaries now.

Tuesday 7th

Saturn the teacher planet and Pluto the transformer planet are sitting together for a week in your communications sector. Issues of control, boundaries and power will come up. This can be quite a struggle for you. Intelligent arguments are the only way to describe this energy and how it will affect you.

Wednesday 8th

Venus, the planet of love and harmony, is in your family sector and can help to soften any tension going on in communication. She will remind you of peace and love, and ask if you will just stop fighting and see the other point of view for a change.

Thursday 9th

Indecision may bother you today. You thought that you had fixed on something, but now seem to be drawn in completely the opposite way. The Moon is in your sex, death and rebirth sector, so you may have trouble bringing things to a close before moving on. Try transforming this rather than throwing it away.

Friday 10th

The first Full Moon of the year occurs in your travel sector. This is also a lunar eclipse. It will highlight family and mothers. What have you brought with you over the last six months regarding these issues? A shadow falls on this now, and something remains undone or incomplete.

Saturday 11th

Travel and education of all kinds will be on your mind today. It is said that home is where the heart is, but you want roots in many places with a special one for solitary retreat. What can you study that may bring you closer to foreign lands, philosophies and cultures?

Sunday 12th

The mighty messenger Mercury joins Saturn and Pluto in your communications sector today. He will gather all the facts and design a course of learning especially for you. You are eager to learn and enhance your career now. Reaching out to others will be your first lesson.

Monday 13th

Before you can really get stuck into the new year, there is one last loving connection you must make. Venus is in the last degree of your family sector, and here will give you a final chance to bring back balance and harmony. Perhaps there has been an argument that you now need to settle?

Tuesday 14th

Venus will glide into your creative sector today. This area also deals with first love and passions. You may find yourself reigniting an old flame or rediscovering a hobby you once loved. Friendship groups give satisfaction now and can support your new learning projects. Listen to their advice and experiences.

Wednesday 15th

You may be beginning to feel emotionally attached to the new agenda you have thought up. This may even become your sole path. Can you make a living and profession from this project you have in mind? Right now, you think that this is indeed possible.

Thursday 16th

Mercury is in the last degree of your communications sector today. He is making sure that you have absolutely all the information you need to proceed with your new learning adventure. However, you may not hear his plea when the Moon is in your dreams sector. Listen carefully.

Friday 17th

Family meetings or gossip will be the theme for the next few weeks. There may be crossed wires, misunderstandings and arguments. On the positive side, Mercury, who is now also in this sector, can make sure that you are all on speaking terms and make an effort to stay that way.

Saturday 18th

Mercury is likely to cause some unrest in your family today, as he is confronting Uranus the disruptor planet. Meanwhile, the Moon has slipped into your sector of self, which can make you moody, melancholic and sensitive. Yet you will likely be quite comfortable like this, and can deal with your darkness now.

Sunday 19th

Your mind will come back to your new projects, and you can inject your current mood into them. This will benefit you greatly as your best learning is done with the Moon in Scorpio. You have more control and self-discipline at these times, even if they are on the dark side.

Monday 20th

The Sun is warming up your family sector today, so any recent tension will now be relieved and antagonists will be exposed. The Moon is meeting Mars, which could pacify someone who still holds a grudge. Anger can be melted into tears now. Be sensitive to others.

Tuesday 21st

Today, you might feel bold and adventurous. Making radical changes appeals now. You are a little rebel, but it is all in good faith and everyone knows that this is who you are. You go your own way and do not take advice from anyone.

Wednesday 22nd

Your recent new ideas, projects and courses of learning are taking up all of your mind space. This could be the making of you. You are very passionate about this new adventure and are putting a lot of time and effort into it. Just be realistic and do not overspend on it.

Thursday 23rd

Relatives and significant others could be in for a shock or a surprise today. It could be uncomfortable and possibly earth-shattering. Your personal mood may inflate and you could become big-headed about your academic abilities. This will annoy family members, and it could be that you are the centre of unrest.

Friday 24th

A New Moon in your family sector will give you the chance to let bygones be bygones and bury the hatchet. Venus and Mars are not playing nicely and will add to any tension between men and women. This will also involve money and love.

Saturday 25th

This is a high-energy day, and you can really get things moving now. The areas affected will be your money and family sectors. There will be a lot of direct communication with tangible results. If you want to sell a car, this is the right kind of energy.

Sunday 26th

You will be able to eke out confidences from people today. Your ability to delve deep and bring up gold is enhanced now. Be sure not to use this to your advantage. You must be a leader of people and show great compassion with anything told to you today. Be discreet.

Monday 27th

Self-expression gets a boost now from planetary energy in your creative sector. This is also a great day for romance, as you will want to drift away with a loved one. Love and dreams can be surreal and you must take care not to drown in illusion. Stay grounded if you can.

Tuesday 28th

How might you put the current floaty energy into your creations? Writing, painting and making something beautiful will take up your time today. Children may also feature, and there will be a general air of laughter and play. Your inner child may come out and mermaids and unicorns will surround you.

Wednesday 29th

You will come back to reality today, and see to your mundane duties. You may have neglected your fitness or housework while you were on cloud nine, so it is now time to attend to the daily grind. You can stay in a fantasy land and be a warrior who gets things done. Is extreme bookkeeping your thing?

Thursday 30th

The push and pull of being human and stuck in the present may annoy you now. You will look to the future and want to be there already. When you look back at the past, you may notice how quickly it has gone. Learn to make the most of the present moment.

Friday 31st

Intellectual pursuits may suffer a setback now, but this is only a passing Moon phase and will not last more than half a day. Take the time off and do something else instead. Something small is out of your control but it is not important, so stop worrying.

FEBRUARY

....

Saturday 1st
The Moon in Taurus will hit Uranus today, so any
dealings with significant others could become volatile.
This influence could also be quite the opposite and
bring pleasant surprises. If it is negative, then you must
refrain from projecting your shadow onto another now.
Do not let that volcano blow.

Sunday 2nd
Women will get the upper hand in love relationships
today. There will be some sweet-talking and coaxing
and they will get their own way. Taking back control and
restoring balance is the nature of the day. Let Venus and
her abundant love and harmony influence your actions.

Monday 3rd
Once again, Mercury is on one of those crucial last
degrees of a sign. This time he is about to leave your
family sector, and will ask you to ensure that any
disagreements and arguments have been smoothed over.
Do not follow an urge to air your feelings and then run.
This will not please Mercury.

Tuesday 4th

Research, communication and analytical thinking may enhance your creative projects today. This is also your self-expression sector, and Mercury's influence will go a long way now. Venus, the planet of love and harmony, is injecting positivity into your new educational courses. She is loosening up some boundaries for you to cross.

Wednesday 5th

Planetary positions will make the air fizz with tension. Conflict between men and women is possible. Action and emotion are at odds. There could be a light-bulb moment, and you may voice an opinion this is revolutionary or controversial. Keep it controlled and compassionate. Put that stinger away.

Thursday 6th

Your travel sector will be lit up today by the Moon joining a point that is referred to as the node of fate. This will have you stretching into the future and possibly dreaming of a home in the sun. Do you have a gut reaction when thinking about this?

Friday 7th

Venus is putting her last-minute finishing touches on subjects you are passionate about. Love affairs will get a spark of harmony and artwork could become inspirational. You may also have a rush of energy and want to transform something that you previously lost interest in. Give this a new lease of life.

Saturday 8th

The Moon will enter your career sector today, giving you the motivation to complete a job. Elsewhere, Venus is entering your health and duties sector where she is the warrior woman. She is on a mission and will see that your time is spent equally between mundane jobs, your health and being of service to others.

Sunday 9th

A Full Moon in your career sector could put you on a pedestal today. You may be the poster boy/girl for your company and be rewarded for a job well done. Try not to let this go to your head. Praise is nice but do not attach your ego to it.

Monday 10th

Your friends and social network will support you today. Connecting to people with the same quirky or deeply esoteric interests as yourself may make you feel less alone, and more a part of a worldwide tribe of misfits. The Bohemian lifestyle suits you best. Philosophise with friends.

Tuesday 11th

You may take pride today in your ability to learn and
absorb new information. This could also be as simple
as being the chatty one in the group. The negative side
of this is that you could also be a gossiper. Counselling
work or psychology can help keep this a positive.

Wednesday 12th

Solitude beckons you. Time spent alone is when you
do your best thinking. The downside of this is that you
often have a tendency to overindulge in rich food. If you
like being alone, enjoy it. If you don't stay away from
what will make it worse.

Thursday 13th

You may feel negative today and put up barriers round
yourself. This means that you may think about rejecting
or quitting any new learning. Do not be so hard on
yourself. When it comes to self sabotage, you are the
master. This is just a passing phase.

Friday 14th

Recent frustrations will settle as the Moon moves
into Scorpio. Put your mind to esoteric or mysterious
subjects. Read a spy novel or take a walk around your
garden at night. Put that recent deep thinking into
something practical now. Be the deep and mysterious
Scorpion everyone recognises. Rise above the naysayers.

Saturday 15th

Mercury is about to go retrograde and this may cause all sorts of trouble. Make sure that your devices are backed up and travel plans are finalised. This will affect your creative and self-expression sector. Unfortunately, this also includes love affairs, so speak only if it is kind, true or helpful.

Sunday 16th

Mars is now joining the other planets in your communications sector. This will add instant energy to everything connected to this area. Your research, learning, speaking and listening abilities will be heightened until the end of March. Mars energy can be brutal too, so refrain from being a relentless workaholic.

Monday 17th

Mercury will begin his retrograde period through your creative sector today. This is the time to review and redo anything that is not quite to your satisfaction. Reorganising your time spent in this area will also benefit you. What is it that needs a makeover? Do a rerun of the last three weeks.

Tuesday 18th

There is a lovely connection today between Jupiter in your communications sector and Neptune in your creative sector. Whenever these two connect, it has a big impact. Dreams can get larger and possibly less realistic. Stay grounded and use this energy to expand your potential for learning and creating.

Wednesday 19th

The Sun is entering Pisces, which means your creative sector will get a boost of joy. This is a light-hearted time that aids empaths, mystics and artists. The Sun will shine light into dark corners and urge you to bring them out into the open. What talents have you been hiding?

Thursday 20th

Today, you may just want to immerse yourself in study. Learning a new language appeals to you now, and this will go very well with any course of study. You may be making short trips to aid your study or the trips may stand alone as the information you seek.

Friday 21st

This is a high-energy day, as Mars and Uranus are meeting. These two unstable planets can bring aggression and violence, but this is a pleasant connection and will aid in moving something forwards that currently feels stuck. The shift will happen in travel, communication and learning. This will be a welcome breakthrough.

Saturday 22nd

More surprises are on their way today. The Sun will add warmth and light to yesterday's connection, and this could feel like seeing a door where before there was only a wall. Families are also in focus. Do something unusual now. Think outside the box and add more surprises to the day.

Sunday 23rd

There is a gorgeous New Moon in your creative sector today. This Moon rules endings, so you can bring something to completion with love. You can also set intentions and affirmations that will help you start something new or put passion into projects that have become boring.

Monday 24th

Jupiter and Venus are locked in a dispute today. These are the planets that endow good things, harmony, luck and love. This is happening in the areas of creativity and new learning, so you will feel the frustration. Use this time to pause and assess what you have done so far.

Tuesday 25th

Do you feel like retreating today? Mars has hit a point in the sky that is about the past. Retracing your steps could help you gain a perspective on where you are going, but this is wasted time. Move on. Keep marching forwards without looking back now.

Wednesday 26th

Mercury is in the glare of the Sun today. Remember that he is also retrograde. This is another day to stop and do nothing. You will struggle to think straight, so nothing will be achieved by pushing it. Do not get drawn into futile arguments today.

Thursday 27th

The frustrating energy continues. If you cannot sit it out, the best thing to do is some exercise. The Moon is in your health sector, Mars is marching on and Mercury is saying nothing. Do some fitness and get back into your body. You could also get out into nature.

Friday 28th

Now you have settled down and emotions are quieter, spend some time with a loved one, a partner or someone who inspires you. This can bring you back to a sense of belonging and connection. A tasty meal or an intimate time will delight your senses today.

Saturday 29th

Mercury has come back to the point where he connects with disruptive Uranus. This could herald a nice surprise, but is more likely to be the opposite due to his retrograde. Struggles around power and control could occur. Manipulation could be a theme too, so be careful.

MARCH
....

Sunday 1st
Take a day off from routine and connect to your
personal interests. The Moon is still in your
relationship sector, indicating that you should involve
others with the subjects you are passionate about. Talk
to them about what is exciting you at the moment. Tell
them what you are up to.

Monday 2nd
If there is someone you can have deep discussions with,
then now is the time to indulge. You will have the energy
over the next couple of days to seek universal truths and
expose anything that does not sit right with you. Secrets
and lies could surface now.

Tuesday 3rd
The Moon is still in your sex, death and rebirth sector.
This influence may make you want to end something.
The trouble is that you could take a long time to decide
if you really want to do this. Once decided, you will be
capable of being brutal and of cutting cords easily.

Wednesday 4th

The recent energy shifts today, leaving you yearning
for something new to explore. Put on your armour and
conquer some new land. Mercury is retrograding back
into your home sector, which means that you need to be
careful and avoid unnecessary criticism of loved ones.
Keep your hand over your mouth.

Thursday 5th

Your emotions and actions are not in sync. An energetic
activity, which seemed like a good idea at the time, is
now disregarded. Staying home and wallowing in a bit of
luxury and good food appeals more. Venus, now in your
relationship sector, will heat things up for you.

Friday 6th

Today, you may resent having to run around and do
small chores. This is one of those days when paperwork
and filing need to be sorted. Resistance to these tasks is
futile, and you will feel better when they are done and
dusted. A bit of self-discipline will get them done.

Saturday 7th

The Moon is entering your career sector today. In order
to succeed, you need to show what you are made of. You
are no shrinking violet in the workplace, and are quite the
force to be reckoned with when on top form. However,
remember that success and respect must be earned.

Sunday 8th

Venus is meeting Uranus today and, as this is happening
in your relationship sector, you could be in for some
disruption. However, this could go either way. You may
experience hostility or romance with your partner. It will
not be a boring time, that much is certain.

Monday 9th

A Full Moon occurs in your social sector today. Look
back at the last six months and see how far you have
come in the area of friends and social networking.
You may now have become someone who is relied on,
respected and trusted. This Moon will also illuminate
false friends.

Tuesday 10th

Mercury finally turns direct today, so travel,
communicating, technology and contracts can be attended
to. See to family issues first and then any creative projects
that may have been affected. Venus, in your relationships
sector, is making plans. She is looking to the past and also
to the future of important relationships.

Wednesday 11th

Saturn will be at a crucial point in your creative sector
for the next two weeks. Ensure that the hard lessons you
have while he is here are fully absorbed and assimilated.
In the meantime, your mood today is dreamy and could
possibly be out of balance. Steady yourself.

Thursday 12th

The Moon is entering Scorpio today, and this is your
monthly time to experience everything around you as
intensely as you wish to. The trouble is, that if it is mild
and boring, you can make it intense. Not everything is as
deep as you would like it to be.

Friday 13th

Scorpions often need to get their hands dirty and
connect with nature, and today is a great time to do this.
You will benefit from following the lead of Taureans by
indulging in food or practical, physical work. Gardening
would be just the thing for you.

Saturday 14th

There is a lot of mixed energy around today, but it is all
good. Dreams and visions will be given an adrenaline
boost by Mars. You will see what needs to be transformed
into a thing of beauty. You are able to be more empathic
than usual and may help someone in need.

Sunday 15th

Mercury is retracing his steps to the critical last degree of your family sector today. Is there anything you refrained from saying whilst he was retrograde? Can you safely and compassionately say this now? Perhaps you need to apologise? Whatever it is, you are now given the chance to say it with kindness.

Monday 16th

The Moon moves into your money sector today, which will get you motivated and looking at your unique skills. What can you do to earn more money? Mercury is back in your creative sector, so there is a good chance that between the two planets you will find a talent and put it to good use.

Tuesday 17th

This is an excellent time for innovative ideas and plans. Uranus, the disruptor, is also responsible for great ideas that can radically shake things up. Think about what skills you may have learnt in the past. Can you use them now to benefit your finances?

Wednesday 18th

Your emotions are tied up with your new learning projects now. Like a dog with a bone, you will not let these things go as they fire you up so much. Short trips for learning, leadership or training purposes are on the agenda. You would do very well to attend.

Thursday 19th

Family matters concern you now. Are you the psychedelic sheep of the family? You may well be the odd one out, but they love you all the more for it. Spread the love and shine your unique light in your home life. There is no one quite like you.

Friday 20th

The spring equinox has arrived, and this is technically the beginning of the astrological year. This is a fantastic time to set intentions and make affirmations for the entire year to come. Tempers could flare with siblings, and past actions may come back to haunt you. You may also assess the nature of your closest relationships.

Saturday 21st

The Moon and Mercury are meeting today in your creative sector. This is also the area of your chart where new love can be created. Discussions could be empathic and somewhat surreal. You will need to be sure of your boundaries now. Keep them healthy and respectful.

Sunday 22nd

Saturn, the old wise teacher, is moving into your family sector today. Think of him like an elder in the family who has literally seen the world and has great teachings to share. Apart from his retrograde later this year, he will be here for two-and-a-half years with huge lessons for you.

Monday 23rd

There are two conflicting energies in the air today. The first is dreamy and delicious, and takes place in your creative sector. The second is between your two ruling planets, Mars and Pluto. This is highly volatile and you could find yourself tearing something down or changing it completely.

Tuesday 24th

The New Moon in your health and duties sector is another chance to make mini resolutions. You can now bring a respectful end to something that is no longer serving you. Starting something new is favoured. Maybe a new routine or just scheduling some time for yourself would be good.

Wednesday 25th

Ask yourself how much time you give to others? Do you feel resentful that nothing ever seems to come back your way? You must decide whether you give yourself unconditionally or if you would like to see favours returned. You may be giving out mixed messages here.

Thursday 26th

Today, you could be extremely emotional. The Moon is moving into your relationship sector and making poor connections to almost every other planet. This is a time to be alone and look at why you feel like this. Your childhood conditioning is the root of your habits, reactions and behaviours.

Friday 27th

Take a duvet day today. Feeling overwhelmed and unable to cope with the outside world is a golden opportunity to make time for retreating. Do what you like doing best. Eat your favourite food and watch your favourite film. Nest and let your inner child be calmed by familiarity.

Saturday 28th

Venus, in your relationship sector, wants to remind you that although you just feel like eating ice cream and watching fantasy films, your intellectual pursuits can nourish you too. Get out your new plans and ideas and maybe do a little light reading. Do not stay wallowing in luxury today.

Sunday 29th

Today, you could play detective and do a lot of research. Your alter ego may become engrossed in the mysteries of life and death. Listen to your inner voice and follow the trail it leads to. You may make a lot of discoveries today. Be pleased with yourself.

Monday 30th

Mars is at the last degree of your communications sector. Whenever a planet is at this crucial point it is asking you to make a last-minute check on recent activities in this area. Go over new plans once more. Do they still have the same appeal?

Tuesday 31st

How far from home do you feel is far enough? Family ties will always be there no matter how far you travel. Is it time to cut the apron strings? Today may also see some aggression within the family with fathers and sons being involved. Authority figures could block progress.

APRIL

. . . .

Wednesday 1st

Today has a misty feel about it. Dreams may seem distant and intangible, and words could be difficult to form. Get whatever is in your head down on paper, for this is the realm of poets and artists. Search the depths of your own soul.

Thursday 2nd

The Moon is entering your career sector today, so you will have no choice but to get to work. Your authority and leadership skills are highly regarded. Knuckle down and get the job done and you will be rewarded with acclaim. You deserve this. The limelight is yours now.

Friday 3rd

Venus will shift into your sex, death and rebirth sector today. Here she is a dark goddess, a priestess and an alchemist. She will add mystery to anything you do. She can be choosy and indecisive, but when she fixes on something she will not let it go.

Saturday 4th

Your creative sector will get another nice boost today. You will be able to access the deepest, darkest waters of the unconscious and produce something grand now. This will also affect your love life and give you the sense of being on cloud nine. Venus and Saturn add ethereal love to the mix. Boundaries can merge now.

Sunday 5th

Two planetary energies are merging today. If there are already issues with power and control, expect them to get out of proportion. Communication, short trips and siblings will be involved under this influence. On the positive side, you may get to grips with something you have been struggling with.

Monday 6th

After yesterday's tension, the Moon is now adding her energy. Friendships and your wider social circle could see power struggles and arguments. Do not put your stinger into this mix, as you could be stirring up a lethal poison that has no antidote. Look after number one now. Check in with your health.

Tuesday 7th

There is even more tension in the air. Mars, in your family sector, is connecting very badly to Uranus in your relationships sector. Both have the power to cause explosions. You must act as a mediator now. Talk to those who are throwing their weight around and try to reinstate harmony.

Wednesday 8th

A Full Moon occurs today in your dreams sector. This is a pivotal point and it is asking you to let go of something that weighs heavily on you. What is stopping you achieving your dreams? Tip the balance and lighten the load. You need your own space now.

Thursday 9th

The Moon is drifting into Scorpio and your area of self today. It is also making bad connections to Mars and the temperamental planet of Uranus. You may feel blocked or out of control. A volcano simmers within you. Keep it simmering. Do not let this blow.

Friday 10th

After yesterday's drama, you can now get back in control of your emotions and have an easier day. You can best deal with this by expressing it in writing or artwork. You, out of everyone, know the gold that is waiting in the dark shadows of your psyche. It can sometimes be your best friend.

Saturday 11th

Mercury will fly into your health and duties sector today. While he is here, he will be asking that you look at your schedule to ensure that you have time for yourself. Starting fitness regimes or just some time out will ensure personal quality time. You have itchy feet now.

Sunday 12th

Connections between your family sector and your duties sector today mean that you must not neglect a family member. You may need to spend time with an elderly person. A telephone call or a quick visit will suffice and show that you are thinking about them. This will be greatly appreciated.

Monday 13th

A passion for new learning will return. Whatever it is that you are doing this year, it has really grabbed you. At this point, you are doing all the research needed to make this something that brings in money. Keep going with this. You can reach the top if you stick at it.

Tuesday 14th

You may have a momentary feeling that you are not in control of this big dream of yours. Is this too big for you? Are you feeling overwhelmed by it? If this is true, there may be a way to bring it down to a manageable size.

Wednesday 15th

Think of a balloon that has been over-inflated and is
ready to burst. This is the energy of the day, and once
more it concerns your communications sector. You or
someone around you may become egotistical, but this is
too much and it will backfire.

Thursday 16th

Your emotions are tied up with family at the moment.
However, the Moon is making a connection to Venus
who is in the area concerned with fishing for secrets and
other people's money. Inheritances and legacies could
be discussed today. You may find some money stashed
away to share between family members.

Friday 17th

Your self-expression will be on top form today. You will
have the gift of the gab, and could persuade others to do
something that interests you. This may also come from
another and you will find that your empath qualities are
called upon. Now is also the time to bring something to
a natural end.

Saturday 18th

Mercury and Venus are talking together today. Mercury
wants to know if you are looking after yourself and Venus
is instructing you on the finer things in life. Mercury rules
trade and Venus rules money, so there is also a chance of
buying and selling. This could be a profitable day.

Sunday 19th

Mercury turns his attention to Mars, who is in your family sector today. Direct and forceful communication may be necessary. The Sun is moving into Taurus, shining a light on personal relationships. How you react with others is under the spotlight now. Be good.

Monday 20th

You could be feeling under the weather today. Take some time out to look after yourself. It is possible that you are close to burning out. Let others see to themselves today because you need some self-care. Stop taking on too much, there are only twenty-four hours in a day.

Tuesday 21st

Nice connections from the Moon to both Venus and Mars make this a great day for romance. General relations between men and women will be easy too. There is equality in the family. Women will be seen, heard and respected for their wisdom.

Wednesday 22nd

There may be some resistance against elders in the family today. Older people are just not in sync with younger ones. This influence can also mean that you are torn between spending time with a lover or family. Is it possible to do both and please everyone?

Thursday 23rd

The Moon is joining the Sun in your relationships sector today, and there is also a New Moon. This is a great chance to renew your connections to special people. A New Moon also gives you an opportunity to make mini resolutions and start as you mean to go on.

Friday 24th

Is there anything that you would like to build? Today's Moon position is like a gardener or builder, and you may want to build a special place for you and a lover. Make plans with good foundations. You cannot fail if you start under this Moon's influence.

Saturday 25th

You may have an irresistible urge to go looking for secrets today. The Underworld is likely to fascinate you now. This is owing to the combined energy of Pluto and his messenger boy Mercury. Sex, death and rebirth are all subjects that grab your attention, and you would like to share this with someone. Be discreet now.

Sunday 26th

Today, Pluto, your co-ruler, starts his retrograde period in your communications sector. Jupiter is giving Mercury a reprimand about his recent snooping for secrets. There could be a light-bulb moment in your important relationships as the Sun lands on Uranus. This could be electrifying or explosive.

Monday 27th

Mercury goes off to sulk in your relationship sector today, and there will be a lot of conversations in this area for a couple of weeks. You may meet someone new and will want to know everything on the first date. Make sure that you share your stories too.

Tuesday 28th

The Moon hits the point of fate today. This is the last time this will happen in your travel sector, so make the most of it and look at where you would like to go, call home or feel nourished. This point can also be about mothering and protecting.

Wednesday 29th

Your intellectual pursuits may fill up your mind now, but you will have no time to spare. You are starting to feel that you have taken on a burden that you cannot carry. You will feel like this for a while, but rest assured this is something you can do.

Thursday 30th

Your career will take centre stage, yet there are rules and regulations you must adhere to. These may be new rules or a change of management structure. You may just be at odds with your boss today. This is a quickly passing phase, so keep your head down.

MAY

. . . .

Friday 1st

The month of May begins with some potentially hostile energy in your relationships. Unfortunately, this will occur in your family and work sectors too. Steer clear of these areas if you can and become absorbed in your studies or simply spend time alone. Instability is the word of the day. Ground yourself with physical activity.

Saturday 2nd

A weekend with friends or groups on social media is just the thing for you now. Friends will appreciate your need to be meticulous and your organisational skills. There is a chance that you will be called upon to help someone through a bad time. Remain open-minded.

Sunday 3rd

Conversations will be easy today. Either you or someone close to you will express some deep emotions. This could also be your significant other. Another way to look at this energy is that you are doing important inner work. You will recognise what needs changing within yourself.

Monday 4th

Mercury has nothing or everything to say today. Thoughts could be muddled and overwhelming. Time spent alone right now will help you focus on yourself and nothing else. Aim for emotional balance. Yoga and meditation will help, junk food will not. Walking in nature will also benefit you today.

Tuesday 5th

There will be a big shift in the collective today, and this influence will last for eighteen months. For you, this means that sex, death, rebirth and shared finances will come into focus. It's time to deal with some or all of these issues. You may not even realise that you are already doing this.

Wednesday 6th

The Moon is drifting into Scorpio today, which means your mood is likely to intensify. Whatever the starting point of your mood, it is guaranteed to get deeper. Knowing you, it will be more on the melancholic side. This is nothing to worry about, as this is your best time to connect with your unique essence.

Thursday 7th

The Full Moon is now in Scorpio. This is one of the most significant Moons of the year, and even more so for you. Personal issues are staring you in the face. They are literally screaming at you and desire that you make big changes now.

Friday 8th

You need to let go of something that has been dragging you down. This could be to do with money, love or your home environment. Something is stopping you from showing your true potential in these areas. Foreign travel attracts you but upsets your bank balance.

Saturday 9th

Mercury is in your opposite sign that deals with important relationships. He is connecting with Pluto today and is helping you make that change. Transform something old into a thing of beauty. This is good Earth energy and can help you ground something into reality. Manifesting what you want comes easily now.

Sunday 10th

Mercury is connecting with Jupiter today, bringing a big Earthy energy. Jupiter rules fortune, religion and is a great planetary influence. Discussions with your partner about shared dreams and visions will have Jupiter's blessings now. Keep talking and listening together. Communication skills with a partner will get much better.

Monday 11th

The wise old teacher Saturn goes retrograde today. Saturn retrogrades can be tough lessons that have come back because you are not learning from them. These lessons involve communications and short trips. The new learning and study you have been interested in is now under scrutiny. This will feel blocked for some months.

Tuesday 12th

Mercury is entering your sex, death and rebirth sector today. The God Mercury could enter the Underworld at will, and this is an area he feels most at home in. Expect conversations, enquiries and research to be of a very deep and esoteric nature. Taboo subjects will interest you now.

Wednesday 13th

Venus will today begin her retrograde period for forty days in the same area as Mercury. This means that, between the two of them, there will be upset and struggle in these areas. There will be dramatic endings of personal relationships. Shared finances are an issue here too.

Thursday 14th

Mars entered your creative sector yesterday. This area also involves falling in love and your self-expression. You may get a boost of energy now but it could also be overly assertive and aggressive. It is best to use Mars' energy in a positive way and put it into your artwork.

Friday 15th

Another planet goes retrograde, and now Jupiter will retrace his steps in your communications sector. These are big, heavy steps and you will need to assess areas where your ideas and plans are just too big. There will be much resistance here, but this is another lesson about over-inflating your ego.

Saturday 16th

The Moon is making her first uneasy connection to retrograde Venus. You may be beginning to feel emotionally detached from someone or something that has previously made you feel passionate and fulfilled. Breathe deeply, this could be an illusion. You may just be overly sensitive and blinded to what is really going on.

Sunday 17th

You need to get some self-control back. Heading to the gym or a wellness clinic could be a good start. Stick to your daily routines as these will give you a sense of normality in what is a very confusing time. Practical tasks will stabilise your emotions now.

Monday 18th

Endings and new beginnings are weighing heavily on you. It is difficult to know what to do for the best. This is a passing Moon phase so do nothing right now. You may feel that you want to unload all your deepest secrets, but you must keep them to yourself.

Tuesday 19th

This is another day where your emotions are just too much, even for you. The Moon is making a nice connection to Venus, but she is not listening. She has her own agenda, and sisterly love is not a part of it. You may reach out, but you are ignored.

Wednesday 20th

The Moon is entering Taurus today, to deal with relationships and your own shadow. You should feel more grounded, but you may also find this difficult at the moment. Do your best to get in touch with your body and your home environment. This will help calm you.

Thursday 21st

The Sun is entering your sex, death and rebirth sector. This will add some warmth to the heavy atmosphere that is there at the moment. It will also shed some light on why these upsets are happening. Follow its rays and you may discover what has been hiding in the shadows.

Friday 22nd

A New Moon happens today in the same area of your life as the Venus retrograde. This is your chance to set intentions and affirmations for the next month. Look at what is going on right now, particularly in relationships. Is there anything you would like to expand on or share?

Saturday 23rd

Self-expression may prove difficult today. You may not be able to say what you are feeling without heavy emotions, such as anger and frustration. This is the day to make messy art, angry poetry or go to the gym. You must release this tension in a creative, harmless way.

Sunday 24th

You should reach out to the wider world today. You could get involved with discussion groups about astrology or other mysteries of life. Listening to lectures about these subjects and connecting with like-minded people will be good for you. See who is out there with similar interests.

Monday 25th

Today, you have a yearning to simply escape. Living away from family is attractive and you see this as a way to find your inner peace. Foreign lands call to you. You perhaps like the idea of being a stranger in a strange land. Content yourself with books or documentaries and escape into your mind.

Tuesday 26th

There is a difficult Moon connection to Pluto, the planet of power and control, today. You feel thwarted in your plans to escape. You may feel as though you have been abducted and held against your will. This is just a brief phase that you must confront every month.

Wednesday 27th

Whenever the Moon passes into your career sector, you
can feel more focused and determined. Setting your
mind on your job and doing your best is one of your
virtues. Be careful that this does not lead to arrogance or
bragging as these do not bring respect.

Thursday 28th

Mercury has finished investigating your secrets and is
now moving into your travel sector. While he is here, you
may enjoy spending time looking at maps, researching
new countries and planning getaways. Mercury likes to
travel and wants you to broaden your horizons now. You
may even feel like settling in another country.

Friday 29th

The weekend has almost arrived and it is time to be with
friends and have some fun. Your social network may be
small, but it is of great value to you. Online groups can
bring satisfaction too. Your personal interests may not be
shared by close friends, but you don't mind this.

Saturday 30th

Are you the organiser within your close friendships? Is
there something you can arrange for you to enjoy with
friends? Your wisdom and skills are sought after now,
and this will give you a boost in confidence. You will
enjoy helping people from your social groups.

Sunday 31st

Today is one of rest for you. The Moon is entering
your dreams sector, so you will most likely prefer to be
alone in your own head. You may feel that no one really
understands what goes on in your mind, but this is okay.
Time spent alone is time well spent.

JUNE
·················

Monday 1st
Press pause and take a day to think about your
projects. There is a lot of retrograde activity in your
communications sector, so this is not the time to charge
ahead. The next few months will be about making solid
foundations for when the energy changes and you are
good to go again.

Tuesday 2nd
This could be an intense day. Beginnings, endings and
deep feelings are in focus. This will be more evident in
relations with the opposite sex and could lead to break-
ups. Remember, Venus is retrograde. Your tendency to
delve deep and seek psychological reasoning could go
against you today.

Wednesday 3rd
The Moon in Scorpio adds depth to your emotional
state today. You may want to express what is on your
mind but fear that this will cause upset. Venus is in the
heat of the Sun and is ready to burn up and rise again.
You can show your phoenix qualities now.

Thursday 4th

You will have a good focus today and will be able to aim your arrows at targets. However, this is likely to make your enemies run, as it is they who are in the line of fire. Use this energy to plant new seeds of thought into a person you have been disagreeing with.

Friday 5th

Today, there is a Full Moon in your money and possessions sector. This will highlight what you have striven for in the last six months. Financial ventures or maybe new home ideas that you planted back then will come to fruition now, one way or the other.

Saturday 6th

The Moon shifts and the focus is now on communications and short trips. You may think negatively about how everything is a struggle for you. Take one step at a time, nothing is ever achieved by jumping ahead. You need to exercise patience and curb the need to hurry to reach the top.

Sunday 7th

Do you sometimes feel as though you are hanging from a cliff? This feeling is because of your sheer determination to do things your own way. You must look around and see that there are those who can make your climb safer. You just have to let them.

Monday 8th

This is the time of the month where you feel most restricted. The Moon is passing those retrograde planets in your communications sector, and you may feel like giving up on new learning goals. This is a rest stop. Look how far you have come so far. Try to enjoy the view.

Tuesday 9th

As the Moon shifts, you will probably need family around you. Even though you may see yourself as unlike them, you understand that blood bonds are very important. You may seek out an older, wiser family member and spend time learning valuable lessons about boundaries. Family stories can bring pleasure now.

Wednesday 10th

Today could bring you a foggy state of mind. What you once thought to be solid truths are now exposed as pure fantasies. This can unsettle you and you may question yourself. Take off the rose-tinted glasses and see things in reality. You may have to make sacrifices now.

Thursday 11th

The Moon drifts into your creativity sector today, bringing you empathy and sensitivity. This is great news for any writing, painting or musical exploits you want to do. This also bodes well for love relationships and self-expression. If you are the artist or appreciate the art of others, this is a lovely energy.

Friday 12th

Today, you will feel the effects of the Venus retrograde more keenly. You are likely to feel sensitive and fragile. A melancholic connection between the Moon and Venus can make you feel very vulnerable now. You must be strong and not give in to codependency as you will regret this later on.

Saturday 13th

You do not have to put up with emotional bullies today. The aggression could be passive, so watch out for anyone trying to manipulate you. This energy can give you the strength to walk away peacefully or cave in and be made to feel small and worthless. Be strong.

Sunday 14th

You will get more energy today. Attending to daily routines will bring satisfaction. Make sure that this is not a distraction tactic used to divert you from deeper issues. Check in with your health today. Doing some physical exercise will make you feel good about yourself, as will starting something new.

Monday 15th

Mercury in your creative sector wants you to connect with people today. He wants you to network and share ideas and values. You are not in the mood to do this and will find it hard to communicate with anyone. Believe it or not, there are people out there who will listen.

Tuesday 16th

As the Moon moves into Taurus, your important relationships will come into focus. How you relate to another is questionable now. You may have had some insight into where your barriers are in developing mature one-to-one relationships. This is always a good signpost to guide you.

Wednesday 17th

Saturn wants to teach you a lesson about listening to your elders today. He has returned to the beginning of your family sector, and is asking that you consider your family of origin and your upbringing. What habits and behaviours have you been conditioned with? What have you developed by yourself?

Thursday 18th

Mercury now goes retrograde. The sign he is in involves mothers, nurturing and home life, so this is tied in with Saturn's lessons for you. The next three weeks will raise issues about your parents and young family life. Travel could be disrupted at this time.

Friday 19th

The Sun is crossing the new point of fate in your sex, death and rebirth sector today. This area also deals with shared finances, so you could be looking at investing in your future. There may be issues of control and change today, but you are on top of it and need not worry.

Saturday 20th

A sensitive Mars in your creative sector makes a nice connection to Jupiter and emphasises your drive to get things done today. You will receive a boost of energy and may even stay up all night to finish projects you are passionate about. Use this energy well. Put heart and soul into it.

Sunday 21st

Today is the summer solstice with a solar eclipse attached to it. However, the longest day has a shadow over it. For you, this means that any issues connected to sex, death and rebirth will be exposed. You will be drawing a line under something now.

Monday 22nd

The Sun and the Moon are in your travel sector. The Sun will shine his light here now and you may return to thoughts of putting down new roots in foreign lands. Unusual religions or spiritualities may call to you and you will be compelled to follow where these lead. Philosophy will also attract you now.

Tuesday 23rd

Neptune, the distant, slow-moving planet, goes retrograde now. Your creative sector will feel this more than any other. You may make sacrifices or fall into old, destructive habits. This will be an introspective time for you. Try to think wisely and limit your actions.

Wednesday 24th

You need to concentrate at work today. Your emotions may be all over the place after Neptune's shift. Work will stabilise you and make you feel useful. You are valued for your leadership qualities now, so do not let your work colleagues down. Be strong, but not pushy. Do not show off.

Thursday 25th

Venus retrograde is over. As the tension lifts, you will be looking around to see if it is safe to come out. There may be some wreckage you have to deal with now. If something or someone has left your life during this time, let them go. This was divine timing and should be honoured.

Friday 26th

Your energy and drive are caught in a crossfire today.
You will be assessing your empathic and sensitive
nature. Where can it get you into trouble? Where are
you overly enthusiastic? Look at past mistakes and take a
lesson from them now.

Saturday 27th

Mars is at the final degree of your creative sector,
meaning you must look at unfinished projects and
decide whether they are still worth your energy. This
can be an emotional wrench. This influence can also
manifest in a short-lived temper tantrum. Tears may
come unexpectedly today.

Sunday 28th

Mars is happier now that he has landed in Aries. For you,
this means that he will give you a boost in your health
and duties sector. This is a great energy to start a new
fitness regime, as you will be more likely to stick to it.

Monday 29th

This is a very frustrating day. You may feel that your dreams and new learning experiences are crashing down around you. This is just a passing Moon phase connecting to all those retrograde planets in your communications sector. Stay calm. This is a time to reflect, not act.

Tuesday 30th

Today, there may be huge struggles or huge change. Pluto, the planet of power and transformation, meets Jupiter, the planet of luck, law and religion. Jupiter enlarges everything he touches. This will affect your learning, teaching and communications. Short trips may be delayed and issues with siblings could also surface.

JULY

. . . .

Wednesday 1st
The Sun is connecting nicely to Uranus in your
relationships sector today, and this will bring a nice
surprise your way. Meanwhile, Mercury is in the heart
of the Sun receiving new information, but he is not
saying anything just yet. A secret surprise maybe? You
may learn something to your advantage.

Thursday 2nd
Your home environment and finances will be on your
mind today. You may want to rearrange your furniture
or buy something nice to add a little feel of luxury to
your home. An exotic touch from foreign lands or a
classic painting could bring you the touch you seek.

Friday 3rd
Saturn rejoins your communications sector today,
which offers a chance to assess any recent learning.
Maybe you need to redo a project. Maybe this project
is not working out for you. You will find your personal
limits on education. Do not take on new things at this
time. They will not satisfy you.

Saturday 4th

An emotional attachment to things that interest you is commendable, but you must not let it rule you. Come back down to earth today and look at facts, figures and deadlines. Share any concerns or difficulties you may be having. Elders or teachers will be there to help you.

Sunday 5th

Today brings a Full Moon and lunar eclipse in your communications sector, which is packed full of retrograde planets, as you are already aware. This will highlight your progress since the beginning of the year. Now is the time to think about what to let go of, if things are getting on top of you.

Monday 6th

Your family sector will get an injection of love and harmony as Venus and the Moon connect to smooth over any recent upset with your nearest relatives. You may be called upon to act as a mediator and put the balance right again. Enjoy this nice time with your loved ones.

Tuesday 7th

Venus is once more moving through the beginning of your sex, death and rebirth sector. Any break-ups that have occurred during her retrograde period can now become make-ups. You could also be picking yourself up and walking on with your head held high.

Wednesday 8th

Today, you will need to put your money where your mouth is. Actions and words will not be in sync, so it is best not to say anything that you cannot back up with action. You may disconnect from people who do not deliver now. Remember that Mercury is retrograde, and this is his influence.

Thursday 9th

Are you feeling sorry for yourself? You may be brooding over events where you have gone unseen or unheard. You could waver between blaming and shaming yourself or another person. Money or investments you share with another may need to be reconciled or debts repaid now.

Friday 10th

Sometimes, you need to learn where you end and another person begins. You may feel as though you have lost a part of yourself that was connected to someone else. This kind of attachment can be toxic. It's time to see a good friend who will be honest with you.

Saturday 11th

Your energy will pick up today, and you may want to make mini resolutions. Making promises to yourself at this time will be useful and you will probably stick to them, for a while at least. Your heart wants to move on with new goals in mind.

Sunday 12th

Mercury goes direct today, allowing some fog to lift.
You will begin to see a situation more clearly and
objectively. Surrender and sacrifice are terms you are
familiar with, but do you realise just how often you do
this? There is no need to compromise yourself. It will
do you no favours.

Monday 13th

As the Moon once again enters your relationship
sector, you will be able to enjoy Venusian desire, love
and luxury. Now is the time to restore harmony in
important relationships. Spoiling yourself with good
food and a sensual environment will lift your spirits
and make you feel at ease. You deserve this now.

Tuesday 14th

The Moon is meeting Uranus, the disruptor, today. Use
this energy wisely. You have an opportunity to surprise
yourself now. Emotional shocks are likely, but these can
be nice shocks too. Mothers and fathers, or men and
women could be in opposition today. There is a fight
for leadership going on.

Wednesday 15th

There is a huge spotlight on a control issue. You or someone in your life has been manipulative and forceful, and now the truth will come out. This is also a golden opportunity to change lead to gold. Something ugly can be transformed and made into a thing of beauty.

Thursday 16th

Your emotions may get into a little twist today, and you could find yourself backtracking on a decision made recently. This is thanks to the familiar being the safer option. Over-analysing can exacerbate this uncertainty. You can be the worst of the zodiac when it comes to over-thinking, so don't become your own worst enemy.

Friday 17th

The Moon and Venus meet in the same spot today, for a sentimental chat about what has transpired in the last few weeks. Deep discussions that come from the heart are likely now. You can talk with someone close about taboo subjects without feeling shame or rejection.

Saturday 18th

Once again, you will be yearning to get away. Your mind will tell you that a new life is waiting in a distant land, yet you are unsure about your ability to set down new roots and make alien lands feel like home. Your rational mind says that you can, but your heart says otherwise.

Sunday 19th

Your thoughts are likely to be distracting today. Mercury is having his say about your ideas around travel. Remember when he was receiving new information? Listen carefully, as now he is choosing to share it with you. Listen to the facts, research all the details and make good choices.

Monday 20th

A New Moon in your travel house is just the catalyst you need to put any plans of travel into action. This is the time to plant new seeds of thought. Set your intentions and make clear goals about your wishes. Mothers will have something important to say to you now.

Tuesday 21st

Your career has a knack of grounding you in reality when your mind wanders too far. Yet you have no idea how much you are valued in the workplace. When you are bad, you can be narcissistic, but when you are good you are brilliant. A true leader.

Wednesday 22nd

The Sun is now following the Moon into your career sector. This month will see a lot of light, heat and joy enter this area. The sign the Sun is in now will also bring out your true self. This is no time to be the shrinking violet at work.

Thursday 23rd

Why not spend some time with friends today? Have you neglected your friends in favour of alone time and introspection? You have a good two-way relationship with most of your friends where you are more than happy to serve each other. This is a great day to reconnect.

Friday 24th

You appear to have learnt a thing or two about personal boundaries recently. Anyone who you may have been involved with in your creative projects may try to push you too far today. You must stand your ground and say "No". At one time this would have made you uncomfortable, not so now.

Saturday 25th

Today, it is time to sit back and reward yourself for the lessons you have learnt recently. Put your feet up and relax with a feeling of balance and harmony within. You have learnt when something is no longer of any use to you or is doing you harm. Well done.

Sunday 26th

Mercury will nudge into your relaxed mood and remind you of future travel plans today. Listen to what he is saying and take note. Not all he says is right for you at the moment, but there is no harm in filing this away for future reference.

Monday 27th

Power struggles may come back to haunt you today.
Just when you thought you had it all sorted, Venus
is trying to delude you again whilst Mars is trying to
sabotage your travel plans. Do not let this get to you.
You are just considering how your plans will fit into
your busy life.

Tuesday 28th

Illusions and delusions may get bigger now, so you
must ground yourself securely in your daily routines
and not get lost in a sea of fog. Find an anchor and
throw it overboard. Practise mindfulness and notice
what you pay attention to. Is this really worthy of your
attention or not?

Wednesday 29th

You should spend time at home decluttering your
environment today. A healthy room makes a healthy mind,
after all. Check your bank balance and, if you can afford
it, treat yourself to a meal at a top restaurant. Satisfy your
taste for the exotic today. A good documentary can help
energise your thirst for knowledge.

Thursday 30th

Watch your words today. You might find that a little white lie turns into something that you cannot control. You may even be lying to yourself about something now. Parents and authority figures are in focus today, and this could be where the conflicts are.

Friday 31st

The Moon is moving into your communication sector, so you may be making short trips and talking to a lot of people today. This is an opportunity to get through your to-do list and complete overdue chores. However, take it easy today. There is no urgency. You will get a sense of satisfaction when you are done.

AUGUST

....

Saturday 1st

Information regarding mothers and fathers may come
your way today, and there could be issues of control
and manipulation. Your travel areas, long and short
distance, are connected here. Also, home and career are
in conflict. You want to get away from people who desire
to control you.

Sunday 2nd

A blazing Sun in your career sector is connecting to
Uranus and causing a riot. You could be throwing your
weight around. You are a great leader in the workplace,
but starting a revolution and calling a strike is not the
way to advance. Keep your head down.

Monday 3rd

There is a Full Moon in your family sector today. This
will highlight any intentions or goals that were set six
months ago. Themes of peace and love, as well as a duty
to mankind and the animal kingdom, come up now. This
is why you were feeling revolutionary yesterday.

Tuesday 4th

There is a tension today, with a thin line between assertiveness and aggression. This is because of a connection between Mars and Jupiter who both make feelings bigger. You may feel like hitting the gym hard and overdoing it. Keep focused on positive results. You may be totally energised or you may become burnt out.

Wednesday 5th

Mercury, the messenger, enters your work sector now. With this influence, you can excel at getting on with the job. You will have new energy and be more interested in gathering and sharing information. Making sure that everything is filed and methodical will be important now. Enjoy it.

Thursday 6th

You are very sensitive today. It is said that feeling everything as deeply as you do is both a blessing and a curse. Your love life is touched by the Moon and Venus now, and the elusive soul mate comes into your thoughts. A melancholic day.

Friday 7th

There is more energy available to you today. Emotionally, you will be satisfied by getting on with daily routines. These will take your mind off deeper thoughts. Venus drifts into your travel sector and brings you the harmony you need now.

Saturday 8th

This is a fabulous day to advance the corporate ladder.
Your heart really is in your work commitments right
now, and this is being recognised by those above you. Be
sure to use Mercury's influence of speech, networking
and research. You are more motivated now.

Sunday 9th

You may have a niggling feeling today, which draws your
attention back to new learning. There is not a lot you can
do about it, however. Acknowledge the feeling and file it
for later. Now is not the time, although it is good that it
still interests you. Keep that passion burning low.

Monday 10th

As the Moon enters your relationship sector, you may
feel something bubbling within you. This could go in
one of two ways. You may start unnecessary arguments
or you may be bubbly and joyful like a small child.
Time spent with someone important will reveal which
way this will go.

Tuesday 11th

A nervous energy may bring out the stinger in you. The
Moon and Mercury are not in sync today, and Mercury
could bring restlessness into the workplace. You have
done really well at work recently, so do not let this
passing Moon phase do anything to jeopardise your
prospects. Sit on it.

Wednesday 12th

A midweek relapse into your deeper thoughts is possible today. Why is there no one around who thinks about the same things as you? You may have one of those days where you contemplate the meaning of life in your head.

Thursday 13th

Your two rulers, Mars and Pluto, are confronting one another, so today will be intense. The people around you need to beware. The worst of you could come out now, and you may frighten people with your insistence on cutting out or ripping down something that you are not satisfied with.

Friday 14th

Self sabotage is the name of your game today. You have worked hard all year on new projects and career, but you are at risk of shooting yourself in the foot. It is almost the weekend, so perhaps you can leave early and vent somewhere safe. Go and write angry poetry.

Saturday 15th

Thank goodness your tantrums are short-lived. Today brings a whole sea of gorgeous planetary energy to calm and soothe you. Home comforts, familiar people, favourite TV shows and good food are on the menu. Absorb all that you can, as you need to fill up that cup of yours.

Sunday 16th

Unfortunately, yesterday was the calm before the storm.
Uranus, the planet of awakening and disruption, goes
retrograde in your relationship sector today. Prepare for
some nasty shocks or pleasant surprises with significant
others. Foundations will be rocked now. Routines will
also be on hold.

Monday 17th

To avoid the storms swirling around you today, you
should content yourself with your career. Simply
attending to the needs of the workplace with a calm
attitude will bring you peace. Work is going well at the
moment, so do not add tension from your private life. It
is not necessary.

Tuesday 18th

Today brings a New Moon in your career sector. This is a
great chance to start new work projects, make new deals
and show off your leadership qualities. You may even
be brave enough to ask for a raise today. Courage and
commitment will go a long way.

Wednesday 19th

The Sun is in your career sector today, and is connecting to points in the sky where we look back at the past as well as forwards to the future. There may be some meetings at work to discuss your advancement. Your ideas and vision are recognised now, and you are highly valued in your workplace.

Thursday 20th

Mercury is now shifting his focus, and is flying into your social sector. This is a fantastic opportunity to socialise and network with people who share the same personal interests as you. You are a keen learner, and with Mercury here you may find some teachers who will become very important to you.

Friday 21st

Emotionally, you may want to be alone to dream and contemplate today. Balance and harmony in all areas of your life fill up your thoughts, and you can consider where something may be out of sync with your best interests. What can you do to redress the balance and bring peace?

Saturday 22nd

The Sun is now following Mercury into your social sector. Think of a busy Internet forum or group call, and you will easily see how this influence could work. You are now a social butterfly and in great demand. Friendships flow with the best of energy, and your diary is full.

Sunday 23rd

The Moon is drifting into your first sector today, which deals with self. Because of the recent energy changes, you will feel proud of yourself and content with most areas of your life. You have plenty of activities lined up to occupy you over the darker months but for now, enjoy the sun.

Monday 24th

Mars is getting a lesson from Saturn today, and this is a reminder for you to check in with your health. Have you been overdoing it recently? Perhaps recent excitement has now left you feeling more tired than usual. Whenever Saturn and Mars connect, it is time to slow down.

Tuesday 25th

Finances may be an issue today because the Moon is entering your money sector. Meanwhile, Venus, who is also connected to money, is opposite Jupiter. This influence could correspond to debt or spending too much on luxury items. Spontaneous purchases could be exciting but may not please the bank manager.

Wednesday 26th

You may have an urge to get away and do some travelling. A holiday could attract you, and you may start planning an exciting itinerary. This may be where your overspending is. Mercury is encouraging Uranus to be radical in your relationships sector. Is this a couples holiday you are planning?

Thursday 27th

Today, you may be unrealistic and idealistic. Venus and Neptune are talking. She can sweet-talk the planet of dreams and solitude into anything. As she is in your travel sector, it seems more and more likely that a dream holiday is on the cards for you.

Friday 28th

You may be assessing all future plans right now. You may do this in relation to your duties and obligations to see if they are attainable. You may feel a little stuck and worry about how to get away. Be sensible, and delegate or finish up pending projects before making further decisions.

Saturday 29th

The Moon is making some confusing connections to other planets today, and feelings of conflict may arise from within you. There may be issues with parents or authority figures that need to be addressed now. You may need a friend to help you organise all that is going on in your head.

Sunday 30th

Home and family are important today. Someone cannot get what they want now and may go off to sulk. Be careful during conversations. Make sure that your meaning is clear, as it is possible that your words could be taken the wrong way and get you into trouble.

Monday 31st

Actions and emotions are perfect friends now, and you will be able to follow through with something you are passionate about. There is a forwards motion, and you feel more positive and assertive. Your confidence will get a boost and you can march onwards. Daily routines are done with the greatest of ease and with time left to spare.

SEPTEMBER

. . . .

Tuesday 1st

Mercury is in the last few days of his stay in your social sector. He is also in a sign he rules. Networks and social media connections need to be checked, and any discord needs to be smoothed over now. Love and projects you are passionate about could bring mood swings.

Wednesday 2nd

Today, there is a beautiful, deeply emotional Full Moon in your creativity sector. This is the Moon of poets and mystics. Dreams will be prophetic now, so take note of them. Here is another opportunity to let something go. Mothers and maternal figures will be in focus under this influence too.

Thursday 3rd

Mercury is receiving a new lesson from Saturn today. This is actually more like feedback for you. These two planets are asking you to ensure that the boundaries between friends are respectful and healthy. You may have given all you have in a friendship and not received anything back.

Friday 4th

A battle of the sexes could occur today. Mars, in your
health and duties sector, does not want to do Venus'
bidding. You, or females around you, will desire to
have their own way regarding travel or mothering,
whilst males will be more concerned with looking after
themselves. Which side are you on?

Saturday 5th

Mercury is making his way into your dreams sector, and
you will most likely desire solitude now. This is like the
underworld of your psyche, where you can switch off
from life. Now is the time to process all the information
you have been gathering lately.

Sunday 6th

Venus is shifting today, making an assertive move
into your career sector. Venus brings harmony and
compassion, so balance in the workplace can be
restored. She also rules money, so this is a good time to
gather some finances for the seasonal spending.

Monday 7th

The Moon is in your relationship sector, but once more
is connecting with Uranus the disruptor. Jupiter is
also poking his nose in. Someone may be rocking the
boat, and this could grow into a much larger issue than
necessary. You may feel overly sensitive today, and as if
things or people are being unfair to you.

Tuesday 8th

As the Moon moves into your sex, death and rebirth sector, you may find that restrictions and blockages are affecting your mood. Under this influence, your desire is to get to the bottom of things but you cannot do this right now. This is very frustrating for you.

Wednesday 9th

Turn your attention to work today, as there is some detective work to do there. This is not a bad thing, but you may have overlooked important details and now have the ability to root them out. Finances you share or have invested in could be in the spotlight now.

Thursday 10th

You may have restrictions occurring in your health and duties sector today. Forward-moving Mars is beginning his retrograde periods and will now retrace his steps. You will need to watch your health, particularly your blood pressure, as aggression and anger will be more likely.

Friday 11th

You will be drawn to travel now. You have big adventures waiting for you and this monthly Moon phase brings them closer to your thoughts. The Sun in your friendship sector is burning away some illusions you have had about people you are connected with. You clearly see the fools around you.

Saturday 12th

There may be more disturbances in your important relationships today. Something could come back and play on your mind. Is there any point in reopening old wounds? When you perceive a slight against you personally you just cannot let it go. Can you?

Sunday 13th

The pressure eases a little today. One of the major planets in your communications sector goes direct again. Jupiter will bring you more luck and joy in this area. You may return to those new learning plans you had at the beginning of the year. You may have even found a guru or a teacher.

Monday 14th

Today's energy is brought to you by the Moon and Venus, who are sitting together and spreading the love in your travel sector. This is maternal, caring and nurturing energy. Where do you feel at home away from your home? Thoughts of a special place will lift your spirits.

Tuesday 15th

The Moon is now drifting into your social sector, and you may start to think of friends past and present. Friends can rely on you to be there for them and you are happy to do this. Where have you acted as a teacher or guide for others? Could you be doing this again?

Wednesday 16th

There may be some conflict between lovers and mothers today. This energy could also be seen as a struggle between your parental figures and your inner child. Old wounds from childhood may surface now. This is good news because they are coming up for healing. Sit with your inner child and listen to them.

Thursday 17th

A New Moon in your social sector means that it is time to connect with people who can help you further your current interests. You may also see this as a time for a new path. You may be feeling introspective now and need a different direction.

Friday 18th

Time alone benefits you now. There may be some emotions rising that are difficult to deal with and you are not the best of company. A lot goes on in your head, but only you can work on this. Connecting to your higher self and practising meditation will help.

Saturday 19th

This could be a difficult day. You are moody and irritable. Think of a cat on a hot tin roof, and that is how you will feel today. Pacing up and down does not help. This is the Moon making tense connections, but they will soon pass.

Sunday 20th

As the Moon moves into Scorpio, you could become selfish. However, you could instead use your best Scorpian qualities to do deep self-reflection. Under this influence, you can do detective work on your own psyche and come up with a detailed analysis of who you really are.

Monday 21st

Your money and belongings are the main topics of the day. There are some important details you need to look at. You may have overspent recently, and are now trying to make it up in some way. Check on finances that you share or have invested with another person.

Tuesday 22nd

The Sun enters your dreams sector today. Although this is the darkest area of your chart, the Sun will light up some areas and show you what needs attention. Light and dark may be opposites, but they need each other in order to exist. You must look at what needs healing now.

Wednesday 23rd

Mercury is connecting to Saturn today, which always means that there is a lesson to be learnt. Mercury is in his last few days of your dreams sector. The recent energy has been about introspection for you. Saturn is reminding you that your empath qualities could be abused. Keep yourself safe now.

Thursday 24th

Today could be volatile and aggressive. You will need to watch your words with someone, as it could turn nasty. Disagreements could escalate into violence of all kinds, so be careful. Be kind, honest and respectful. If you need to, simply walk away from angry people.

Friday 25th

You will be pulled back to learning, teaching and short travels today. Earlier in the year, you became attracted to learning something that can enhance your career. This will start to pick up now. You may be travelling to a college or to clients. Internet and email courses are also possibilities now.

Saturday 26th

As it is the weekend, could you spend time with family today? The Moon is settling in your family sector, making this a favourable day for family fun. You may have a quirky family with some unusual characters who can make this a light-hearted day of laughter.

Sunday 27th

Mercury is done with your dreams sector and is asking you to put yourself out there now. You have done a lot of thinking recently and now it is time to put that into speech. There is something you would like to say and people will want to hear it.

Monday 28th

You may be very creative with words today. If you have a project to do or just a piece of writing you would like to produce, do it now. Mercury and the Moon are making a great connection, which will support and enhance your literary skills. Be evocative and romantic.

Tuesday 29th

This is another great day for getting on with things. Saturn now turns direct, and teaching and learning, even small lessons, will be beneficial. With Jupiter and Saturn both back, your communications sector can thrive. Use this powerful energy to get back on track.

Wednesday 30th

There will be one small niggle today as Mars wants to speak to Saturn. Your daily routines and health need a check-up. Mars retrograde is having an effect on your personal wellbeing. You must look at which routines are necessary and which are not. You must drop something for the time being.

OCTOBER

. . . .

Thursday 1st
October begins with a Full Moon in your health and
duties sector. With Mars currently retrograding there,
you should now be able to see clearly how your time is
separated. This opportunity is also great for making mini
resolutions to spend more time on your self and your
personal goals.

Friday 2nd
Venus is moving into your social sector today. This is
good news in the run-up to the festive season. There will
be more harmony now between friendship factions. She
is also insisting that you balance time for friends and
time for you. Expect a lot of dining out whilst she is here.

Saturday 3rd
The Moon and Taurus are making a lovely Earthy
connection today, which will help you to feel grounded.
This may feel alien to you, but stick with it. You may find
a new love within your social groups. This influence will
also show how you split time between lovers and friends.

Sunday 4th

Today, you may find that your heart and head are not in sync. Mercury is in Scorpio and wants to think and talk deeply, whilst your emotional body just wants to be cared for by sensual things like love, food and money. This may cause some unrest within you.

Monday 5th

Pluto, your secondary ruler, turns direct today. This is like a deep breath out, and you should feel the tension leaving your body. This means that all the planets in your communications sector are up and running. Education, trips and new learning experiences are getting the green light now.

Tuesday 6th

The Moon enters your sector of sex, death and rebirth. Endings and beginnings are foremost in your mind. You have the ability to transform something rather than throw it out completely. This is a skill of yours, if you do not let emotions guide your thinking.

Wednesday 7th

You will need to watch your words today. This will involve important relationships and lovers. Mercury in your own sector of self is opposite the planet of disruption. Alternatively, this influence may make you come up with something ingenious.

Thursday 8th

You will be thinking again about travel and settling elsewhere in the world. This is just a whim at the moment, but may turn into something more concrete when Mars is direct again. Your roots are important, but you have a yearning to set down new ones in foreign lands.

Friday 9th

Mars and Pluto, your planetary rulers, are locked in a dispute today. Mars, who represents your energy and drive, will lose. This may manifest as a control issue, which will leave you exhausted. This is a sign to look after yourself more and to get your energy levels back up to normal.

Saturday 10th

There may be a lovely surprise for you today, as Venus is sweet-talking Uranus in your relationship sector. He is in a sign that she rules, so he will listen. Expect to be spoiled or do the spoiling today. It is the weekend, so what are you waiting for?

Sunday 11th

There is no need to be a Sunday worker today. If there is something that needs to be done for your boss, do it at your own pace as your lover or an important person wants to spend the rest of the weekend with you. Put the work down and get back to playing.

Monday 12th

You will be able to concentrate on your work today, as the Moon is entering your career sector. As you already had work on your mind yesterday, you are motivated and know what needs to be done. Colleagues will look to you for advice and feed on your motivation. You are in good spirits.

Tuesday 13th

The Sun is shining directly on Mars in your health and duties sector today. Take this as a neon light that you are doing too much. This is the reason your health has been suffering lately. Let something go, and lighten your load. Even Mars cannot move forwards again with too much on his shoulders.

Wednesday 14th

Just when you thought it was all plain sailing, Mercury goes retrograde in Scorpio. In your area of self, this will be about your own psyche. He will go back into deep, dark corners and reassess things he thought he had dealt with.

Thursday 15th

The energy today suggests that you may have trouble with someone trying to undermine you or steal your glory. This is also about reviewing your communication and education, and asking yourself if this is really what you want. Can you do this? Stop doubting yourself.

Friday 16th

A New Moon in your dreams sector highlights that
Scorpion need for intensity and mystery. You may now
make intentions and affirmations to work more on
your inner self. You are no stranger to psychology and
spirituality, and have a knack for combining these two
together. You will do well at this.

Saturday 17th

This could be an intense day where emotions simmer
like a volcano ready to erupt. You may have an irresistible
urge to say what is on your mind and in your heart. This
will almost certainly result in a lava flow or an earthquake,
and you must be prepared for the consequences.

Sunday 18th

You may feel quite rebellious today. You have great
teachers in front of you, but you have found your own
voice and done your own research. You may be pushing
boundaries with elders. This is all part of the learning
experience and a good teacher will recognise this.

Monday 19th

You may feel extremely tired today. Mars and Venus are
in connection with Jupiter, who makes everything bigger.
Mars is exhausted and Venus is putting more and more
tasks his way, via Jupiter. Have a day indoors and in your
own familiar environment. Eat and sleep well.

Tuesday 20th

Do you remember that Mercury is currently retrograde? This is an unstable time for everyone, and he may be rocking the boat in your relationships now. Mercury issues are usually about misunderstood or cruel conversations. Watch out for this, and do not be the one speaking words that hurt.

Wednesday 21st

The Moon is settling into your communications sector today, so your learning activities will take up some of your time. This is something that you are really putting your heart into and is fast becoming a labour of love. Venus is busy transforming social acquaintances into educational allies. You will soon have a support team.

Thursday 22nd

The Sun is moving into Scorpio today, making this your birthday month. You may feel tired and not really in the mood to do your educational activities, nor your regular duties. Do what you can but reserve some energy for what excites you.

Friday 23rd

Families are featured today and may give you a break from routine. A friendly family get-together sounds like a good idea, but Mercury retrograde may want to say the wrong thing and risk upsetting someone. Keep it light and carefree. There is no need to rake up the past.

Saturday 24th

New friends and allies on your learning journey
will become important now. These could be people
from groups on social media or people you have met
physically. All are valuable and can point you in the right
direction with your new interests. Learn from each other.

Sunday 25th

Mercury is lost in the glare of the Sun, and is saying
nothing for once. Use this time to think and not speak.
This is a receptive, passive time rather than one to share
what you know. Process the new information you have
received recently before overloading yourself. Make sure
there is room in your head for it all.

Monday 26th

A poetic Moon is making sweet connections to the
Sun and Mercury, who are both in Scorpio. It also has
a stabilising effect on anything that could disturb the
status quo. Make the most of this energy. Although you
thrive off drama, this peace will fill your soul.

Tuesday 27th

Dreams and visions could get a boost now. Using
symbols and metaphors will come easily, and you will
be able to put these to good use. Explorations of the
psyche, your education and creative projects all benefit
from this influence. You are quite the poet now.

Wednesday 28th

Today, your dream sector is bookended by Venus, entering at the beginning, and Mercury, flying into it backwards. Love, peace and harmony are added to your solitude and peaceful moments. Enquiry and conversation enhance your shared time. Connection to a divine source is possible now.

Thursday 29th

The Moon is meeting up with a weary Mars in your health and duties sector today, which could leave you feeling emotionally drained. There may also be a feeling of guilt about duties you have neglected recently. Do not feel guilty. This area is draining and you have done the best you can.

Friday 30th

Your relationships and the important people in your life need attention now. This will be beneficial if you have a mutually receptive partner. Otherwise, this will add to the energy loss, and may make you feel worse. Put your other interests to one side.

Saturday 31st

A Full Moon occurs today in your relationship sector. This is the second Full Moon in a calendar month and is known as a Blue Moon. It will highlight the imbalance in love relationships. You will be more moody than usual. Make sure that your needs are met.

NOVEMBER

····················

Sunday 1st

The veil falls and you can see a situation for what it really is now. All the mist and illusion will be burnt away and you will be left staring at the real thing. This will come as a big shock. The question is, what are you going to do about it? The choice is yours.

Monday 2nd

Your attention will shift today, and you will now be probing the whys and wherefores of recent events. You have had a shock to your system, but you will not let things go. You begin a psychological analysis of the circumstances that lead you to be involved with a certain person.

Tuesday 3rd

Emotionally, you will be balanced today. Venus is busy bringing you peace in your alone times and Mars is quiet for once. Attending to the daily grind will give you some stability. You may be called upon to mediate a situation. If this is your situation, make no judgements until all sides are presented.

Wednesday 4th

Mercury is turning direct in your dreams sector today,
so you may need some time to yourself for the next
few days. Reflect on what has transpired during his
retrograde period. This part of your chart rules endings.
You may bring something to a close now and you can do
it with love.

Thursday 5th

You are thinking seriously about travelling or settling
elsewhere now. Be mindful that this influence is not
owing to recent events, but is a passing Moon phase in
your travel sector. Do not make any rash moves right
now. Venus is butting in and also discouraging you.

Friday 6th

You may feel despondent about your education and
learning activities today. Resentment is hanging over
you like a cloud, and you may feel as if you are stuck. Lie
low and take the time to pause and reflect. Do not beat
yourself up about this situation.

Saturday 7th

You need a distraction today, so may have brought work
home for the weekend. Your natural instinct is to make
good use of time. Quietly working away at unfinished
projects or those you have neglected will bring a greater
peace. Prepare to rise above it all like the other Scorpio
symbol, the eagle.

Sunday 8th

This could be a tough Sunday for you. There is a lot going through your mind, but the energy of the Sun and Moon will not allow for progress. This is like a stalemate move in chess. What happens now? Nothing. The game has to end.

Monday 9th

Recent tensions will return today as Venus and Mars move opposite each other. This elaborates on the stalemate situation of yesterday. It's a 'me and you' or 'us and them' stand-off. Men and women will be in power struggles now. This is also about how you present yourself and how you hide.

Tuesday 10th

Mercury is on that critical last degree of your entire chart today. This is about a closure where there can be no going back. You must process what is in your head now, once and for all. Mercury will leave the very deepest point of your chart with clear instructions on how to proceed.

Wednesday 11th

Today, you will realise how the educational activities that have interested you all year can be your way forwards. You have been looking for a vocation that is inspirational. You can make this into your soul's purpose and become a leader. This is worth the hard work.

Thursday 12th

Today will bring refreshment and new insight. The Moon and Venus are meeting in your dream sector, and will uplift you. Mercury is ready for his new mission in your sector of self. Jupiter and Pluto are making huge changes in your communications sector. You will see many positive transformations now. Things are looking up.

Friday 13th

The Moon is entering Scorpio, and this is when your best work can be done, and you can connect deeply to almost anything you are passionate about. The Moon will meet Mercury, and your heart and mind will be in sync. This is the best news.

Saturday 14th

You can breathe deeply again. Mars has now turned direct, so forwards motion, assertiveness and motivation will return. This is a great time to begin a new fitness regime. In fact, this is a great time to begin anything at all and the chances are that you will stick at it.

Sunday 15th

A New Moon in Scorpio offers the chance to recommit to working on your inner self. The only person who can reach your depths is you. The skill set to do this is part of what makes up the Scorpian personality. Make intentions and affirmations now.

Monday 16th

There may be some conflict within you today. This is
about you doubting your own abilities to be successful
with your chosen goals. Trust that this is meant for you,
and that the right path has finally shown itself. Venus is
in her element in your dreams sector. Love, money and
stability are possibilities now.

Tuesday 17th

There are times when you look back at how far you have
come. This is one of them. If you are doing the necessary
self-development, then skills learnt in the past can be
used again now. You may get some genius ideas today.

Wednesday 18th

Do you feel that you have taken on too much? This is quite
normal for you, but know that you can do it. Hesitation
may creep in, so you will need more motivation. This is
going to be a big step into the unknown, but you are no
stranger to exploring foreign territory.

Thursday 19th

You will be able to conquer yesterday's self-doubt,
allowing your heart to fill with passion again. Wise
teachers are making themselves known to you now.
Learn what you can from others who have walked this
path before you. Find a way to make this journey unique
and own it. Step outside your comfort zone.

Friday 20th

As the Moon enters your family sector, you may face resistance from family members today. There may be a lot of discussion concerning your individuality within the group. Maternal figures will show concern, and may attempt to veer you away from your path. This is their way of showing their love for you.

Saturday 21st

The Sun will leave Scorpio today while Venus will enter it. Your money sector will get an energetic boost, and light will shine on any areas that need attention. Venus will restore your sense of self-worth and bring you more peace. Your new journey will be set now.

Sunday 22nd

You may want to finish up old projects now. Romance is in the air, but that air needs clearing first. You could be in love with creative pursuits. A new quest is beckoning and you will be compelled to follow. This is typical of you, ever the seeker, the eternal student.

Monday 23rd

The Moon is making some delightful contacts today, which will make you feel as light as a feather. Everything looks positive, and you may ask yourself if this is too good to be true. Just enjoy the feeling and stop sabotaging yourself. Good things are coming your way.

Tuesday 24th

Mercury is whispering across to Neptune now. He is telling the planet of dreams what the new plans are. Make sure that you have no illusions about your new journey. Mercury can be somewhat of a magician in Scorpio, but you can use this energy to manifest your desires and ground them in reality.

Wednesday 25th

Before all great heroes begin their quest, they need to check that they are strong enough. Now would be a good time to visit the health centre and get general check-ups done. You may need extra vitamins or support to be on top form.

Thursday 26th

You will have a day where you just cannot gather the energy you need. However, do not be disheartened by this. The Moon is sitting on top of Mars, and he is unable to move today. The weight of your emotions can sometimes overcome your energy and drive. Stick with it, this will soon pass.

Friday 27th

If somebody told you not to do something then what would you do? Of course, you will do the opposite, won't you! Today you may be digging your heels in or having a little temper tantrum. This is a day for you, so do not let anyone else dictate your actions.

Saturday 28th

You may fall back into a dream world and create a fantasy land in your head today. Your mind may wander, but this is fine. Be mindful that there is a real world and an imaginary world. Try not to be too unrealistic now as you will only be disappointed later on.

Sunday 29th

Today, you can show people what you are made of. You will want to talk to others about your new plans, but be careful that you do not go over the top and brag. Try not to come across as egotistical. You could be overly talkative now.

Monday 30th

A Full Moon occurs in your sex, death and rebirth sector today. What is being illuminated now? What has come to completion from six months ago? A partial eclipse throws a shadow over the Moon, suggesting there is something lurking in a corner that you may have forgotten about.

DECEMBER

. . . .

Tuesday 1st

Mercury is entering your money sector now. With a bit
of luck, his role as the planet of merchants will help
with a bit of buying and selling. You may want to buy
items for your home environment that have a touch of
the exotic about them. This could be fun.

Wednesday 2nd

As the Moon drifts into your travel sector, you may
realise a few things. Your interest and educational
pursuits are an exploration that is personal to you.
Mercury adds his influence and lets you see how far you
travel in your mind. Make your home and learning your
new travel adventures.

Thursday 3rd

You may feel duty-bound today. There is no time for
dreaming now, and you must simply get on with things.
You could be feeling a little unwell but do not worry,
this is a payback for all the adrenalin you have been
using lately. Home comforts will help you feel better.

Friday 4th

Have you thought about asking for a raise at work? Mercury is making a great connection to the Moon in your career sector today, and he will lend you the gift of the gab. Do not forget that he is in your money sector, so this is worth a try.

Saturday 5th

The recent energy will lift today, helping you to march along with your head held high. There may be some disruption in your important relationships that may affect your working day. The important other may be someone in work, so be warned that this unrest could come from both areas.

Sunday 6th

Venus will give your self-worth a boost today. She is reminding you that you do not have to make sacrifices to get ahead. She is allowing you to dream big and go after what you desire. Her connection to Neptune is emphasising this. Love may be on its way.

Monday 7th

Your social sector will get some attention today. There could be some nice surprises within your friendship groups. How about starting the festive season with a get-together with someone you have not seen for a while? Social media groups could also bring some fun revelations and unconventional thinking.

Tuesday 8th

Saturn is at the critical degree of your communications sector today. He will be here for ten days, so it is time to learn a very important lesson. This is likely to be about personal boundaries and how much you take on. Think hard about this issue now.

Wednesday 9th

The Sun in your money sector is burning away any illusions that you may have had regarding finances. Perhaps you have been overspending and thought this was okay? This is a time when the bank balance needs to be checked before splurging on unnecessary items of luxury.

Thursday 10th

Venus is in Scorpio today, where she is sweet-talking Pluto. The result is that females will be able to get what they want, and will be able to control situations normally dominated by the men in their lives. There will be a light-hearted feel in the air and much laughter.

Friday 11th

Today, there is a lot of movement and activity. The Sun in your money sector is connecting to Mars in your duties sector. This is looking like an expensive season for you. There may be a battle between you and an important person, probably a partner. You are not on the same wavelength today.

Saturday 12th

The Moon and Venus join up today, and the energy is overtly feminine. Venus is the witch or the sorceress in Scorpio and here comes the priestess Moon. Today can be a very sensual day. Be sure to make the most of it.

Sunday 13th

As the Moon moves into your money sector, you may feel a little guilty about your spending habits lately. However, this does not stop you wanting to make your home into an exotic paradise or a Renaissance art gallery. You may bring your foreign pleasures to your own space and create a new comfort zone.

Monday 14th

There is a New Moon in your money and possessions sector today. Mercury is also at the same spot, and he is giving you ideas to use as affirmations and intentions regarding this sector. Is he urging you to spend or save? Does he want you to buy or sell?

Tuesday 15th

Venus is leaving your area of self today, and wandering into your money house. As she rules money, this could be a time of gain or even more luxury spending. There is work to be done in your health and duties sector, and Mars gets on with the daily routine to avoid spending.

Wednesday 16th

You have a vision of where you would like your new work to go. Self-control is the attitude you must approach to ground this in reality. This is your project and therefore no one can understand it the way you do. You are on top of it now.

Thursday 17th

This is an important day, as the Moon is making great connections with those planets that have been dominating your communications sector. Firstly, Jupiter fires up your passion and brings you luck. Then, the Moon drifts into your family sector and meets Saturn who blesses you with self-discipline.

Friday 18th

Today, Mercury is in the heart of the Sun in your money house. You must sit quietly and listen to the information he is receiving now. This will be important for your finances and your home environment. Is there anything more that you need to collect or research in this area?

Saturday 19th

Jupiter is spending his last day in your communications sector. Think of this like Santa Claus coming early and hiding a gift somewhere. The bringer of joy and luck is bestowing you with good karma before he moves on to another area of your chart. You will find that gift now.

Sunday 20th

This is another important day, as Jupiter meets up with Saturn. This is happening right at the beginning of your family sector. Fathers and sons will feature greatly. Other paternal figures or heads of authority may have a confrontation or a blessed reunion. Feel the love here.

Monday 21st

The winter solstice arrives now. Both the Sun and Mercury enter your communications sector and pause for reflection before the wheel of the year turns and the days start getting longer. This is a time of rest before the busy festive season. Look back at the year you have had and give thanks.

Tuesday 22nd

You will have already felt the rush of excitement as the Moon passes into your health and duties sector, but you must now make sure that all jobs are completed before the Christmas break. Make sure that your health is good, as this season may drain your resources.

Wednesday 23rd

There may be a battle of wills today or simply a rush to get things prepared for the festivities. Somebody wants to take control of the whole proceedings and will not accept help. If you must opt out and let others get on with it, do so.

Thursday 24th

Spend some time with your lover or another special person today. The Moon is in Taurus and you could find this energy tense. If you are alone, be good to yourself. You do not have to see anyone if you would rather be alone.

Friday 25th

As the Moon meets up with Uranus, the planet of disruption, hopefully the surprises will be good ones. Mercury wants to have his say in your communications sector and, true to form, he has you making a lot of short trips. This could be a busy Christmas Day for you.

Saturday 26th

The calm after the storm brings a much warmer and quieter energy. The busy day has been and gone, and you can now just sit quietly and feel in total control. Sharing this time with someone special will bring even greater satisfaction.

Sunday 27th

You will have time to reflect now. However, this will not be on a superficial level knowing you. You want to analyse the year behind you and eke out the reasoning behind the more difficult moments. Learn to let it go. That door has closed. Stop thinking of the ifs and buts.

Monday 28th

You will be better able to shift your focus now to the year ahead. There will be much teaching, learning and sharing of information. Your intellectual pursuits will bring you an acclaim you never thought you would have. You have surprised yourself, but now prepare to surpass yourself. Give yourself some credit.

Tuesday 29th

Today, there is a Full Moon in your travel sector. At one time, getting away was all you could think about. You now realise that reading books, watching documentaries or researching other cultures can bring you all the travel adventures you require. Your inquisitive mind is your travel guide.

Wednesday 30th

Mercury is in opposition to the Moon today, and is reminding you that you actually do have the ability to make a career around your persistent studies. Venus has you spending too much again. You may even be falling in love now. Just stay grounded and remember that you have great work to do.

Thursday 31st

Venus is joining a point where you can look back at the past today. Long-lost loves may come back into your mind yet disappear again quickly. You are feeling whimsical and ready to see the year out with love, peace and harmony. Happy New Year!

Scorpio

PEOPLE WHO
SHARE YOUR SIGN

PEOPLE WHO SHARE YOUR SIGN

····················

Scorpios have seduced our screens for decades, from Scarlett Johansson to Goldie Hawn, so it's no wonder that they have a reputation for being the sexiest sign in the zodiac calendar. The Scorpion is a mysterious creature that has brought dark depths to the world in the form of Martin Scorsese's films of the macabre and transformational wonders in the form of RuPaul and his Drag Race. Discover which of these intriguing Scorpios share your exact birthday and see if you can spot the similarities.

October 24th

Shenae Grimes (1989), PewDiePie (1989), Eliza Taylor (1989), Drake (1986), Wayne Rooney (1985), Katie McGrath (1983), Roman Abramovich (1966), Malcolm Turnbull, 29th Prime Minister of Australia (1954), Kevin Kline (1947)

October 25th

Rylan Clark-Neal (1988), Ciara (1985), Katy Perry (1984), Phaedra Parks (1973), Craig Robinson (1971), David Furnish (1962), Chad Smith (1961), Pablo Picasso (1881), Johann Strauss II (1825)

October 26th

Emilia Clarke (1986), Seth MacFarlane (1973), Tom Cavanagh (1968), Keith Urban (1967), Uhuru Kenyatta, 4th President of Kenya (1961), Dylan McDermott (1961), Rita Wilson (1956), Hillary Clinton (1947), Jaclyn Smith (1945)

October 27th

Kelly Osbourne (1984), Marla Maples (1963), Simon Le Bon (1958), Luiz Inácio Lula da Silva, 35th President of Brazil (1945), John Cleese (1939), Sylvia Plath (1932), Roy Lichtenstein (1923), Theodore Roosevelt, 26th U.S. President (1858)

October 28th

Frank Ocean (1987), Troian Bellisario (1985), Matt Smith (1982), Joaquin Phoenix (1974), Julia Roberts (1967), Matt Drudge (1966), Bill Gates (1955), Caitlyn Jenner (1949)

October 29th

Tove Lo (1987), Ben Foster (1980), Tracee Ellis Ross (1972), Gabrielle Union (1972), Winona Ryder (1971), Rufus Sewell (1967), Kate Jackson (1948), Richard Dreyfuss (1947)

October 30th

Janel Parrish (1988), Clémence Poésy (1982), Ivanka Trump (1981), Matthew Morrison (1978), Nia Long (1970), Gavin Rossdale (1965), Diego Maradona (1960), Timothy B. Schmit (1947), Henry Winkler (1945)

October 31st

Willow Smith (2000), Frank Iero (1981), Vanilla Ice (1967), Rob Schneider (1963), Peter Jackson (1961), John Candy (1950), Zaha Hadid (1950), Michael Landon (1936), Sardar Patel, 1st Deputy Prime Minister of India (1875)

November 1st

Penn Badgley (1986), Aishwarya Rai (1973), Jenny McCarthy (1972), Jeremy Hunt (1966), Anthony Kiedis (1962), Tim Cook (1960), David Foster (1949), Larry Flynt (1942)

November 2nd

Nelly (1974), Stevie J (1971), David Schwimmer (1966), Shahrukh Khan (1965), Warren G. Harding, 29th U.S. President (1865), James Knox Polk, 11th U.S. President (1795), Marie Antionette (1755)

November 3rd

Kendall Jenner (1995), Colin Kaepernick (1987), Gabe Newell (1962), Dolph Lundgren (1957), Kate Capshaw (1953), Larry Holmes (1949), Anna Wintour (1949)

November 4th

Jessa Seewald (1992), Dez Bryant (1988), Guy Martin (1981), Bethenny Frankel (1970), P. Diddy (1969), Matthew McConaughey (1969), Ralph Macchio (1961), Kathy Griffin (1960)

November 5th
Virat Kohli (1988), Kevin Jonas (1987), Alexa Chung (1983), Luke Hemsworth (1980), Danniella Westbrook (1973), Famke Janssen (1964), Tilda Swinton (1960), Bryan Adams (1959), Kris Jenner (1955)

November 6th
Kris Wu (1990), Emma Stone (1988), Conchita Wurst (1988), Taryn Manning (1978), Thandie Newton (1972), Rebecca Romijn (1972), Ethan Hawke (1970), Kelly Rutherford (1968), Mohamed Hadid (1948), Sally Field (1946)

November 7th
Lorde (1996), Bethany Mota (1995), David de Gea (1990), Elsa Hosk (1988), David Guetta (1967), Joni Mitchell (1943), Albert Camus (1913), Marie Curie (1867)

November 8th
Jasmine Thompson (2000), Lauren Alaina (1994), Jessica Lowndes (1988), Erica Mena (1987) Tara Reid (1975), Tech N9ne (1971), Gordon Ramsay (1966), Bonnie Raitt (1949), Alain Delon (1935)

November 9th
French Montana (1984), Caroline Flack (1979), Nick Lachey (1973), Eric Dane (1972), Lou Ferrigno (1951), Carl Sagan (1934), Hedy Lamarr (1914), Muhammad Iqbal (1877)

November 10th
Mackenzie Foy (2000), Kiernan Shipka (1999), Zoey Deutch (1994), Taron Egerton (1989), Josh Peck (1986), Miranda Lambert (1983), Diplo (1978), Eve (1978), Brittany Murphy (1977), Ellen Pompeo (1969), Hugh Bonneville (1963), Neil Gaiman (1960)

November 11th
Tye Sheridan (1996), Vinny Guadagnino (1987), Philipp Lahm (1983), Leonardo DiCaprio (1974), Calista Flockhart (1964), Demi Moore (1962), Stanley Tucci (1960), Kurt Vonnegut (1922), Fyodor Dostoevsky (1821)

November 12th
Anne Hathaway (1982), Ryan Gosling (1980), Gustaf Skarsgård (1980), Tonya Harding (1970), Nadia Comăneci (1961), Megan Mullally (1958), Hassan Rouhani, 7th President of Iran (1948), Neil Young (1945), Grace Kelly (1929)

November 13th
Matt Bennett (1991), Devon Bostick (1991), Gerard Butler (1969), Jimmy Kimmel (1967), Steve Zahn (1967), Whoopi Goldberg (1955), Chris Noth (1954), Frances Conroy (1953), Andrés Manuel López Obrador, President-elect of Mexico (1953), Robert Louis Stevenson (1850)

November 14th
Russell Tovey (1981), Olga Kurylenko (1979), Travis Barker (1975), Gary Vaynerchuk (1975), Josh Duhamel (1972), Run D.M.C (1964), Patrick Warburton (1964), Charles, Prince of Wales (1948), Astrid Lindgren (1907), Claude Monet (1840)

November 15th
Paulo Dybala (1993), Shailene Woodley (1991), B.o.B (1988), Sania Mirza (1986), Lily Aldridge (1985), Jeffree Star (1985), Chad Kroeger (1974), Jonny Lee Miller (1972), Jimmy Choo (1948)

November 16th
Pete Davidson (1993), Vicky Pattison (1987), Gemma Atkinson (1984), Maggie Gyllenhaal (1977), Paul Scholes (1974), Brandi Glanville (1972), Missi Pyle (1972), Lisa Bonet (1967), Sheree Zampino (1967)

November 17th

Tom Ellis (1978), Rachel McAdams (1978), Lorraine Pascale (1972), Jeff Buckley (1966), Jonathan Ross (1960), RuPaul (1960), Danny DeVito (1944), Lauren Hutton (1943), Martin Scorsese (1942)

November 18th

Nick Bateman (1986), Fabolous (1977), Anthony McPartlin (1975), Chloë Sevigny (1974), Owen Wilson (1968), Kirk Hammett (1962), Elizabeth Perkins (1960), Kim Wilde (1960), Linda Evans (1942)

November 19th

Tyga (1989), Adam Driver (1983), Jack Dorsey (1976), Jodie Foster (1962), Meg Ryan (1961), Allison Janney (1959), Charlie Kaufman (1958), Calvin Klein (1942), Larry King (1933), Indira Gandhi, Former Prime Minister of India (1917)

November 20th

Michael Clifford (1995), Oliver Sykes (1986), Future (1983), Andrea Riseborough (1981), Kimberley Walsh (1981), Ming-Na Wen (1963), Sean Young (1959), Bo Derek (1956), Joe Walsh (1947)

November 21st

Conor Maynard (1992), Colleen Ballinger (1986), Carly Rae Jepsen (1985), Jena Malone (1984), Nikki Bella (1983), Ken Block (1967), Björk (1965), Nicollette Sheridan (1963), Goldie Hawn (1945), René Magritte (1898)

November 22nd

Hailey Baldwin (1996), Alden Ehrenreich (1989), Oscar Pistorius (1986), Scarlett Johansson (1984), Boris Becker (1967), Mark Ruffalo (1967), Mads Mikkelsen (1965), Jamie Lee Curtis (1958), Rodney Dangerfield (1921)